Poetry & Compassion

Poetry & Compassion

———

Essays on
Art
&
Craft

Frederick Smock

WIND PUBLICATIONS

First edition

International Standard Book Number 1893239535
Library of Congress Control Number 2005937648

Front cover art by Guy Davenport. From *50 Drawings* (Dim
Gray Bar Press, 1996)

Acknowledgments

Some of these essays were previously published, sometimes in a variant form, in the following papers and journals:

The Filson Quarterly— "Kay Boyle on the Côte d'Azur"
AWP Writers Chronicle— "Poetry & the Elegant Solution"
The Courier-Journal— "Poetry & Politics," "Poetry & Compassion," "Poetry & Danger," "Late Auden," "Keats, Revised"
The Louisville Review— "Nocturnes on a Drainpipe"
The Merton Seasonal— "Pax Intrantibus"
The Merton Annual— "Poetry & Exile"

"One Writer's Beginnings" was published in *Savory Memories* (University Press of Kentucky, 1998).

to Olga-Maria

Contents

Poetry & the Physical

Anyone with a cursory knowledge of Archibald MacLeish can usually quote the final couplet of his famous poem, "Ars Poetica"—

> *A poem should not mean*
> *But be.*

Which is ironic, because the rest of that poem argues against this kind of abstract summation. Instead, he insists on the primacy of the image, vivid in its description and in its emotional intensity—

> *A poem should be palpable and mute*
> *As a globed fruit.*

The word "poem" comes to us from the Greek *poieia*, meaning *to make*—a made thing. I am intrigued by the idea of the poem as a thing separate from us, a work of art separate from its maker, like a sculpture, or a bowl. A thing in its own right, that has its reasons.

A poem, having a physical being, having a sculptural shape on the page, inhabits a body. Is sensual. This is not a new idea. Others have commented on this:

1) Lawrence Durrell wrote about "the broken torso of the poem," a phrase which also suggests that a poem has been aged in the poet's mind to its mythic completion;

2) A poem's presence in our lives is not merely conceptual. Poetry is not just ideas, not just communication, but, as Borges reminds us, it is a passion and a joy. Such emotions cannot exist without a covering of skin;

3) All art, Walter Pater wrote, aspires to the condition of music—because, in music, form and substance cannot be separated.

A poem does not enter the reader's body only through the brain, but also through the eyes, skin, gut, heart, feet.... Therefore, a good poem cannot come from the brain alone. It is not a linguistic puzzle, as many of us were taught in high school. Rather, a poem depends on the senses, all six or eight of them. The reader's intellect makes sense of the poem, but the intellect cannot *sense* the poem. And a poem is nothing if not sensual. We talk about poems intellectually, but we do not *experience* them intellectually.

The poet Howard Nemerov wanted to "see in a thinking way," and thereby to "make some mind of what is only sense."

The mind is not the only, and maybe not the central, apprehender of truth and beauty. A writer "bodies forth" a poem. A reader gets chills, goose-bumps. The experience of poetry asks us to be fully aware, in an almost animal way. This is one challenge of poetry.

Here is a poem that offers a lot to appreciate physically, James Wright's "Lying in a Hammock at William Duffy's Farm in Pine Island, Minnesota" —

Over my head, I can see the bronze butterfly,
Asleep on the black trunk,
Blowing like a leaf in green shadow.
Down the ravine behind the empty house,
The cowbells follow one another
Into the distances of the afternoon.
To my right,
In a field of sunlight between two pines,
The droppings of last year's horses
Blaze up into golden stones.
I lean back, as the evening darkens and comes on.
A chicken hawk floats over, looking for home.
I have wasted my life.

Notice how carefully he notices in this poem. Not a *yellow* but a *bronze* butterfly, noting the late angle of the sun, and emphasizing the butterfly's classical beauty and, at the same time, by contrast, its great fragility. A *black* trunk—on the shadow side of the tree. Not *cows* but *cowbells*—deep in the hammock (and Jim Wright was a heavy man) he would not have seen the cows, and to say that he could would be dishonest; he can only hear the cowbells. "The droppings of last year's horses / blaze up into golden stones"—he can even make horse shit look pretty! He recognizes that the bird floating overhead is a chicken hawk. It is important to know the names of things. I am always made confident in writers who know the names of plants and animals.

The ancient Chinese philosopher Kung Fu Tze (Confucius) said, "All wisdom is rooted in learning to call things by the right name."

Writing a Poem

When the sculptor Leslie Hawk died suddenly, in June of 1997, her friends faced a daunting challenge—in the midst of grief, to come up with a service to commemorate her life. Leslie was strenuously anti-religious, so it could be no traditional funeral, and no priest or minister could be allowed to preside at this event. Yet her passing had to be observed in some special way, for she was a remarkable individual. We decided that each of us would be responsible for a portion of the service, and my part was to write a poem.

Under normal circumstances (and what are those?) the writing of a poem can be difficult enough, except for those times when a poem comes unbidden, and reasonably well-formed. Such times are rare. (Of course, the unbidden poem has been gathering itself, for a while, like a storm cloud just off the horizon; it only bursts suddenly, with all the sweetness of rain.) But the present circumstances were abnormal.

I despaired of writing a worthy poem in only two days' time. Anxiety is not a productive state. And I was working against several personal taboos—by writing hurriedly, out of a store of private knowledge, and under the sway of great emotion. For a day and a half, I thought hard about Leslie's life, her work as a sculptor, her log-cabin house. I cast about wildly for ideas, and wrote many a dreadful line. Then suddenly this came to me in a flash, in a single block of inspiration:

> *Looking out the back window of her cabin,*
> *beyond her garden, and the pines,*
> *beyond the barn and the animals on the lawn—*
> *an elephant, a dragon, a bear—*
> *the hill falls away to the lake,*
> *the lake gives way to the woods,*
> *the woods fall away into the distance.*
> *The eye is drawn to the long prospect,*
> *to the inevitabilities of the landscape,*
> *the artist's far perspective.*
> *But I want to call your attention to her garden,*
> *the plants in their rows, carefully staked*
> *or trellised. Lettuce leafing out,*
> *tomatoes ripening in the sun, asparagus*
> *rising out of their dark earthen beds.*
> *Notice that the garden has no fence, only a gate.*

And there the inspiration ended.

Her garden did, indeed, have no fence, only a gate. The deer might come and nibble freely on her flowers and the shoots of new vegetables. But any person wanting to visit her garden had to enter through the gate. This was one of Leslie's rules, and she enforced it strictly.

The gate, by the way, she made herself, out of thin bars of wrought iron welded together. She was a metal sculptor. She made tall angular people, and busted-open bird cages, and gates. The

5

bars on her gates were plenty wide enough for small animals to pass through.

Anyway, her poem, clearly, was not yet finished. Even if it was just one more line, that gate had to do something, didn't it? But what?

It became a heavy symbol to carry around all afternoon. I thought furiously. Sitting at my desk, I coined many weighty last lines, invoking the gates of Paradise on down to the gates of the underworld, and not one of them worked. Finally, I decided to go out to her place, to her farm, in hope of finding the right frame of mind.

My experience at her farm, that evening, reminded me that looking is more important than thinking, sometimes, in the writing of a poem. For when I got to her place, I walked about in the yard, and eventually came around the side of her house to the garden, and there I plainly saw before me the last line of the poem:

Notice that the gate is standing open.

Poetry & Unknowing

In high school, we were taught that a poem is a puzzle. Find the hidden meaning, and you get an A. No wonder Billy Collins says that high school is where poetry goes to die.

Poems are not written to be discussed in classrooms. Nor are they written to provide ready answers for life's troubles and woes. More often, this writer believes, poems are written to ask questions.

The Romanian poet Lucian Blaga believed that poetry aims to deepen the mystery of life. Science will explain the world to us; but poetry—like childbirth, like love—reminds us just how inexplicable the world is.

Borges went so far as to say, in his 1967 lectures at Harvard, "When I am writing something, I try not to understand it. I do not think intelligence has much to do with the work of a writer."

Art is comfortable with what it does not know, or, with what it knows only in part. A poem often begins in wonderment, and widens the circle, like a boy stirring his finger in a pond.

Here is a little story by way of illustration: The physicist Niels Bohr was giving a talk about atomic energy—this was in the 1960s sometime—and he had drawn on the chalkboard the now-familiar diagram of an atom. The poet Stanley Kunitz was in the audience, and asked, "Is that really what an atom looks like, or is it a metaphor for what we know so far?" Bohr did not have an answer for him.

Because writing is an act of discovery, it can begin with the known, but, at some point, must venture into the unknown.

"Most poets," Mark Strand has written, "are drawn to the unknown, and writing, for them, is a way of making the unknown visible. And if the object of one's quest is hidden or unknown, how is it to be approached by predictable means?"

So much of the writer's work happens within the subconscious, before the conscious mind receives the first draft, which we call inspiration. Some of the writer's work happens within the heart, too.

Here is a little poem by the Norwegian Olav Hauge that maybe illustrates this point:

> *Year in, year out, you've been sitting bent over books,*
> *you've been gathering more knowledge*
> *than is needed for nine lives.*
> *When it comes to the point,*
> *so little is needed, and that little*
> *the heart has always known.*
> *In Egypt, the god of knowledge*
> *had a head like an ape.*

To know is to be certain of what has gone before. It is also important for us to think about what has not happened, what might happen, what may never happen. I am thinking here of Milan Kundera's comment, in *The Unbearable Lightness of Being*, "Our dreams prove that to imagine—to dream about things that have not happened—is among mankind's deepest needs."

Poetry & Method

I.

Artists evolve peculiar methods. Sometimes they do so out of necessity. Hemingway wrote standing up, in later life, because of a bad back. Proust, a neurasthenic, wrote lying down in a cork-lined study. Maya Angelou locks herself away in a hotel room in order to gain the required concentration.

Sometimes they do so out of a curious choice, perhaps a superstition, to court the various muses. D.H. Lawrence climbed around in mulberry trees naked—the rough bark excited his imagination. The poet Marianne Moore lay in a coffin she kept in her New York City apartment, staring at the ceiling, not infrequently puffing on a thick Cuban cigar.

The German author Fredric Schiller kept a drawer of rotting apples in his desk; whenever he felt his inspiration flagging, he pulled open the drawer and took a strong whiff of the emanating fumes. (As it turns out, rotting apples release nitrous oxide, a stimulant to the brain, as well as an evocative aroma.)

Ancient Roman poets bathed in strawberries.
Voltaire wrote on his lover's naked back.
(Notice that nakedness recurs as a theme here.)
John Cheever, modest fellow, wrote in his boxer shorts.

A thousand books have been written about how to write a poem. While they are all useful, up to a point, one must acknowledge that every writer evolves his or her own method— what works peculiarly for them. And this wisdom is not transferable. Methods can be modeled—and they are always interesting—but they cannot be copied.

In every issue, *The Paris Review* runs an interview or two with writers or translators, and, among other things, they are asked to talk about how they work: Is the desk at a window? In a corner? What talismans (fetishes?) share the desk? Is clothing optional with you? What time of day or night do you write? Do you drink coffee or tea? Something stronger? Each writer describes his or her own method. I find these revelations fascinating. Chiefly, what I have learned from these interviews has to do with the courage to write, and with the worthiness of the act.

Each writer must find his or her own method.

The speaker in Billy Collins' poem "Purity" takes a pot of tea into the study, closes the door, takes off his clothes,

> *Then I remove my flesh*
> *and hang it over a chair.*
> *I slide it off my bones*
> *like a silken garment.*

Then he removes his organs, and at last is ready to begin. "I am entirely pure: nothing but a skeleton at a typewriter."

Radical nudity, indeed.

II.

My younger son played soccer in middle school. He and his teammates were all thin and tanned, with bowl-shaped Kobi Jones haircuts, and, when they stood backlit on the pitch, it was nearly impossible to tell them apart. But when they began to play, to run around, I could pick out my son by the way his body moved.

"The rhythm is the person," poet Marianne Moore observed.

For a poet, that rhythm is discovered and revealed through language. The way one writes is as distinctive as the way one walks or talks. A line of Seamus Heaney's carries his linguistic DNA, so to speak—"All along the dank, sunk, rock-floored lane...."

Even this one phrase is recognizably different from, say, Billy Collins, whose poem "Dharma" begins with the lines,

> *The way the dog trots out the front door*
> *every morning*
> *without a hat or an umbrella,*
> *without any money*
> *or the keys to her doghouse*
> *never fails to fill the saucer of my heart*
> *with milky admiration.*

Who differs equally from the Taoist poet Jane Hirshfield: "By daybreak, the soundless mountains bow under snow."

The rhythm is the person.

At the front end of the writing process, a poem comes together when the rhythms come right. The poet searches for the rhythm of words that is uniquely his or hers.

"Of its own accord," said the confident Ovid, "my song would come in the right rhythms, and what I was trying to say was poetry."

Every poem carries within it instructions for the reader about how it is to be read. Likewise, every poem carries within it instructions for the writer about how it is to be written. The poet discovers these only as the poem gets written. In other words, every poem comes with its own rules. And, sometimes, these rules must be broken in order for the poem to get written.

Here we find some of the excitement and difficulty of writing.

"You have somehow to know the sound that is the exact sound: and you do in fact know, without knowing how," Wallace Stevens observed. "Your knowledge is irrational."

The poet William Stafford used to get up before dawn and sit with pencil and paper by a window looking out into the darkness, waiting. And eventually, he said, something always came along. They weren't always keepers. But when they came right, they bore the unmistakable sound of his inner voice—

> *The stars have died overhead in their great cold.*
> *Beneath us the sled whispers along. Back there*
> *our mother is gone. They tell us, "If you hold on*
> *the dogs will take you home." And they tell us never*
> *to cry. We'll die too, they say, if we*
> *are ever afraid. All night we hold on.*
> *The stars go down. We are never afraid.*

Poetry & Politics

War is a failure of the imagination.
– William Blake

One afternoon I returned to the leafy campus of my alma mater, after so many years. It was a quiet return, at twilight, for an evening poetry reading. An autumn wind blew through the tall oak trees in the quad. I had a little while to sit outside on a bench and think back over the several lifetimes survived to reach this moment. The sun began to drop down behind some trees. A few students laughed loudly as they crossed from building to building. The squirrels, who are unusually trusting on college campuses, scampered about near my feet in the sparse grass, busying for the winter.

That week there had been rumors of war—true, as it turned out. Driving over to campus, I was stopped by a train pulling miles of flat-cars loaded with army trucks of every description, almost toy-like in their block shapes and uniform greens-and-blacks. Like the toy trucks I played with as a child—the little jeeps and tanks with moveable gun turrets and convoy trucks that I drove over the dangerous roads in my grandmother's braided living-room rug. A child, toying with extinction.

Then I noticed the army transport airplanes, flying low and ponderous toward Fort Knox.

Rain had fallen earlier in the day, and cleaned the sky to a heart-breaking blue. We came to hear poems. Hungry souls drifted toward the library auditorium. This was time taken out of our busy schedules, but it was not time taken out of our lives. Listening to poems is time given back to us, time added onto our lives. On days such as this, we realize again what an eminently sane thing it is to stop a while and listen.

Reading, that night, and listening to others read, as the light withdrew behind the dark maples, I became aware of the sky going black behind the tall windows of the room, slowly giving us back in wavy, glassine reflection. We were outside ourselves, looking in. A people stilled by voices. Sometimes, this is the best we can offer—a meditative stillness, a rapt attention.

It is a political act to read a poem. Though I might wish otherwise, though I might wish that a poem be only that, a poem, I am also aware of how it creates a counter-motion—to haste, to unfeeling and unthinking. At a poetry reading in Westchester, New York, just days after the World Trade Center attacks of 9/11, Stephen Dunn read only love poems. They worked as a counterweight to the recent tragedy, in no way obscuring it, but simply adding to the moment a voice that spoke intimately of the beautiful.

Still, I wonder, why must art so often be considered within the context of politics? Politics is so little considered within the context of art.

Poetry & Danger

My student Abbie writes to me from Sarajevo, where she has gone to give a poetry reading. Her first book has just been published, and an American friend of hers with the World Bank is flying her over.

She sends me a postcard of the Sarajevo library building—the National and University Library of Bosnia—a golden-brick palace on the left bank of the Miljacka river. She writes, "On August 25, 1992, Serbian troops set it on fire and in three days more than 2,000,000 books burned. People ran into the building and carried out armfuls of smouldering volumes over and over. Now the windows are boarded up and it's inhabited by pigeons, mostly."

She has been warned by her Bosnian friends to stay on the paved walkways—the city and its surrounding countryside are still littered with land-mines—and to tame her golden hair. She will punch out at least one man during her stay.

Repression is where you find it.

When the Mohammedans sacked the famous library at Alexandria, in 640 AD, a half-million texts were destroyed, by using them as tinder for the bathhouses of the captured city. Even so, it took six months to burn them all.

The Nazis burned and looted Jewish libraries and museums. As Heinrich Heine observed, "Where they have burned books, they will end in burning human beings."

15

The American Library Association keeps files and a website on bibliocide—the willful destruction of books and archives—detailing this "loss of memory." Their policy manual quotes Supreme Court Justice William O. Douglas, bravely saying, in 1953, at the height of the Red scare, about the burning of books related to Communism, "Restriction of free thought and free speech is the most dangerous of all subversions. It is the one un-American act that could most easily defeat us."

Libraries have been purposely destroyed during Charles VIII's invasion of Medici Florence, during the Spanish Civil War, the Japanese invasion of Manchuria, the Taliban wars in Afghanistan, and countless other conflicts, including the most recent war in Iraq.

Books burn slowly, and the 2003 fire that destroyed twenty million or so documents in Baghdad's library and national archives was not an accident of war—the Wall Street Journal reported that this fire was started by white phosphorus, a fast-burning substance favored by militias specializing in disposing of paper documents. This library held much of the pre-Baathist Iraqi history, and U.S. officials did nothing to stop the conflagration.

Demagogues tend not to prefer an enlightened populace.

Poets and intellectuals—who are paid little, and who are usually ignored by the general population—have this consolation, at least: they are the ones the tyrants go after first.

In the picture postcard Abbie has sent me, the terraced river, a deep sapphire-blue, flows serenely between the library in bright sunlight on the left bank, and, on the right bank, a snowy pathway underneath a chiaroscuro of tree branches, where couples walk arm in arm. Nothing looks amiss.

Abbie will return safely, and bring me a souvenir from Sarajevo—a ballpoint pen made of an old shell-casing. Swords into ploughshares! This pen will almost get her arrested in three airports.

I write these words with the pen she brought me. The brass of the old shell-casing fits snugly against the second joint of my trigger finger.

Poetry & Compassion

There is a famous story about the French poet Robert Desnos. Interned by the Nazis, he and his cellmates were lined up one morning at a train siding to be sent to Auschwitz and certain death. As they waited, under the watchful eyes of the guards and their dogs, one old man asked Desnos to read his palm. Given the circumstances, this might have seemed a grim request. But Desnos complied. He took the man's hand in his own, and said aloud to him, "You will live a long life and die happy." The old man was elated.

Other men in the queue came up to Desnos, asking that their fortunes also be told. To each one, Desnos told the same fortune: "You will live a long life and die happy."

The mood of the morning changed; even the Nazi guards became of a lighter spirit. When the train arrived to take the men to Auschwitz, the guards no longer had the heart to follow through. Instead, they marched the men back to their barracks, where they lived out the war.

What might this story mean? For one thing, it means that Keats was right when he spoke about the "truth of the imagination"—the imagination is a real and active force in the universe. For another, it speaks to the generous nature of the poetic impulse.

Poetry, like all imaginative works, "replaces indifference with attention," in the words of Guy Davenport. Indifference doesn't mean not caring, it means not caring *one way or the other.* Indifference is apathy—a disengagement from the world. This differs from detachment, of course, which is an ironic or a zen *attach*ment to the world.

At the most, perhaps, poetry teaches "tenderness toward existence," in the words of Galway Kinnell. Call it an active caring for the world, in thought or action. And I can think of no good reason to privilege the benefits of action over thought. A monk who prays for the world does no less than the protester out on the barricades, or the volunteer in a children's ward.

Immediately after the 9/11 attacks, the virtual airwaves of the internet were crowded with the flights of poems around the globe, trying to make sense of this new world, and to give comfort in the aftermath of unforeseen tragedy. (We should remember that tragedies comparable to 9/11 happen often in other places around the world, and always have; we should not think that we are unique, or special, only because we are unused to such things.) One of the oft-cited poems was Seamus Heaney's "The Cure at Troy," whose chorus reads, in part:

> *Human beings suffer,*
> *They torture one another,*
> *They get hurt and get hard.*
> *No poem or play or song*
> *Can fully right a wrong*
> *Inflicted or endured.*

Having acknowledged the limitations of the arts, he goes on to transcend those limitations, by calling down a hope for some kind of grace:

. . . hope for a great sea-change
on the far side of revenge.
Believe that a further shore
is reachable from here.
Believe in miracles
and cures and healing wells.

This is some of the good work that a poem can do—provide a measure of hope and compassion for the world.

We can trust poetry. As Mary Oliver wrote, "No poet ever wrote a poem to dishonor life, to compromise high ideals, to scorn religious views, to demean hope or gratitude, to argue against tenderness, to place rancor before love, or to praise littleness of soul. Not one. Not ever."

Poetry & Prejudice

The U.S. Treasury Department—which, among other things, handles cases of treason—recently warned American publishers against translating poetry from Iran. Such translation, they vowed, would be considered "trading with the enemy," punishable by fines and jail time.

This event was brought back to me today by the sight of a Hummer, in front of me in traffic, sporting bumper stickers that read "Bomb Mecca," and "The Only Good Arab is a Dead Arab."

How are these two events related?

The enforcement of ignorance, in the first example, leads to the endorsement of prejudice, in the second.

In other words, how might the driver of that Hummer profit by reading Arabic poetry?

How might he (for I assume it was a "he") profit by reading, say, the 13th-century Sufi mystic-poet Rumi? One of Rumi's great themes was the affirmation of universal brother- and sister-hood, as in this untitled poem:

> *I want to hold you close like a lute,*
> *So we can cry out with loving.*
> *You would rather throw stones at a mirror?*
> *I am your mirror, and here are the stones.*

Or the modern Iraqi poet Abdula Peshew, the last stanza of whose poem "Fratricide" reads, in part:

> *Two dead bodies lie there,*
> *brothers they were.*
> *They shared the same dream,*
> *but they differed in color.*
> *The distance between them*
> *is bridged by*
> *the burning sighs of a mother and father.*
> *As for their leaders,*
> *they are enjoying themselves*
> *in merriment and mirth.*
> *The gap between them is judged by*
> *the enemy's dining tables*
> *with glasses of wine.*

The world is webbed with sympathies which ordinarily we cannot see. Poetry—art—operates extraordinarily in that it lays bare these connections (sometimes painfully, if it's not what we want to hear).

A philosopher friend of mine likes to talk about natural law theory, which emphasizes human flourishing. The basic idea, as she puts it, is that things like knowledge, friendship, art (aesthetic experience), even life itself are intrinsic goods foundational to the well-being of all persons, both at the level of the individual and community.

According to natural law theory, one way to judge the morality of an action, attitude, or policy, is to reflect on whether—and to what extent— it promotes flourishing of being in general.

Neither the attitude of the Treasury Department, in this instance, nor that of the Hummer driver, leads to human flourishing. Rather, these attitudes work against knowledge, friendship, art, life itself.

Poetry & Silence

The poet's job is not to speak, but to listen, so that things will speak through him or her.

This is not an argument against prolificacy. Po Chu-I wrote a thousand poems in his lifetime. Shotetsu wrote thirty thousand. Issa wrote ten thousand poems just about insects. Hurrah, we say—they listened well!

Silence is a necessary pre-condition for sound. Silence surrounds and shapes sound. In the way a composer says that a symphony relies upon the silences between the notes? (And sometimes, as in John Gage's famous symphony, silence *is* sound!)

Our popular culture militates against silence—even companionable silence. Television, telephones, tele-portation devices of all kinds insist shrilly upon our attention, keeping us skating across the surfaces of our lives. But what of the depths? Only the quietly reflective mind can think deeply.

Writers I know seek out the silences of Gethsemani and St. Meinrad abbeys, where the quiet is punctuated only by the silver tones of bells calling out the progress of the day. At my house, a neighboring parish bell begins the day at six a.m., with nine bells for the Angelus, in groups of three with a pause between each. The pauses— the silences between each set— let me hear the bells more clearly, of course.

"A single stroke of the early prayer-bell wakes me," Tu Fu wrote. "Does it also waken my soul?"

In the film *"Touts le Matins du Monde,"* Gerard Depardieu plays a 17th-century cellist. Because the film wants to love its music, it has no background music or noise, only an absolute silence against which you can hear individual water-drops, footsteps on gravel, cello notes, with a startling clarity.

Poems, like music, begin and end in silence. The way a poem shapes—and is shaped by—its own silence is important to the poem.

Thousands of years ago, Yang Wan-li wrote, "Get rid of words and get rid of meaning, and there is still poetry." What did he mean by that? Beyond the words, the heart and spirit of the poem anticipates the reader.

Back of many poems, there breathes a palpable silence, like the silence of great forests, as in this poem by Tristan Tzara:

> what is this road that separates us
> across which I hold out the hand of my thoughts
> a flower is written at the end of each finger
> and the end of the road is a flower which walks with you
> Lee Harwood, trans.

In a way, the words on the page are not the poetry; they are the occasion for poetry. Poetry happens when a reader's gaze lifts the words off the pages. All of this is enacted in an attentive silence.

Witness this poem by George Trakl:

> At evening, the sound of the cuckoo
> stops in the wood.
> The grain bends lower,
> the red poppy.

Black thunderclouds bloom
above the hill.
The ancient song of the cricket
fades off into the fields.

The leaves of the chestnut
trees stir no more.
Upon the spiral staircase
your dress rustles.

One silent candle shines
in the dark room;
a silvery hand
extinguishes it;

No wind, no stars. Night.
                    Robert Genier, trans.

What is the answer to that old riddle, If a tree falls in the forest and no one is there to hear it, does it make any sound? The answer is No; it makes (as in a poem) the opportunity for sound.

Writing a Ghazal

It disturbs me greatly that my country has taken to serial bombing of Arab nations. As of this writing, the U.S. has been bombing one Arab nation or another for nearly twenty consecutive years. We also demonize our enemies, as if to support our often spurious rationale for going to war. Over the years, we have demonized the Indians, the Mexicans, the Germans, the Russians, the Koreans, the Vietnamese, the Grenadians, the Afghans, the Iraqis, etc., all the while confusing the governed with the governors.

When I edited *The American Voice*, a literary journal out of Louisville, I published a poem by Paula Gunn Allen, a Laguna Pueblo-Sioux-Scottish-Lebanese-American, which I would like to quote in part, in this context:

> *They tell me that in Beirut*
> *men lounge around the tables*
> *over thick syrupy coffee*
> *and recite poetry.*
>
> *Not ones they've made themselves,*
> *but everyone's poems.*
> *These are people who know*
> *poems are word in flesh, incarnate....*

Not only are our Arab brothers not demons, they are an ancient and highly cultivated tribe. We—the U.S.—destroy them in our own ignorance, and at our own peril.

So, every semester, as a small act of conciliation, I ask my students to write ghazals, that venerable Arabic form of poetry. We work backwards into the ghazal. (It's pronounced guzzle, but my students want to say gazelle.) We begin with its formal requirements. We schematize the poem, then work backwards into narrative and meaning. Form becomes not merely a stricture, but another way of tapping into the subconscious. A ghazal is traditionally written in couplets, with the same word or phrase repeated at the end of each couplet, and a rhyming word preceding the phrase. Sounds easy, when it's first assigned. On the due date, however, my students often have found an appreciation for the form.

One student, Janell Oliver, wrote this ghazal of mourning, which I reproduce here with her permission.

FORGOTTEN

I don't know how to mourn for you anymore.
It's been five years, Dad. That's a long time anymore.

Your closet's been emptied out, your truck sold,
we don't even live in the same house, same town, anymore.

Those antique records are stuffed in trunks in the attic—
George Jones and Merle Haggard aren't popular anymore.

The leather jacket, limp on the hook, has lost your smell,
your boots are no longer molded to your feet anymore.

I no longer sleep with your urn beneath my bed,
I hardly ever speak your name anymore.

All you are is a forgotten joke I think I've heard before.
In the mirror all I see is Mom's face anymore.

I am an Oliver, but what is—who is—an Oliver?
I don't even know what that name means anymore.

The Secret

I tell my students, the secret to writing is this: *the right word in the right place every time*. Class dismissed.

That of course was Flaubert's formula. *Le mot juste*. And he lived every day of his writing life in "fear of the false," as W.G. Sebald phrased it, in his book *The Rings of Saturn*, "which kept [Flaubert] confined to his couch for weeks or months on end in the dread that he would never be able to write another word without compromising himself in the most grievous of ways."

My students laughed, then they got serious.

There is an inner call to truth and justice that makes every writer a moralist, at least about his or her own work. And the consequences of a bad day writing can be dire, like a stain on the soul. It can't be laughed off. You cannot drink it away, though some try. This is the other side of the elation a writer feels when things are going well.

"The misuse of language," Socrates averred, "induces evil into the soul." Well, Socrates was an absolutist, and he was speaking here about the sophists who deliberately twist language to suit their agendas, public or private. But writers feel the shame of which Socrates speaks, and feel themselves impugned when their writing disobeys or, worse, betrays them.

There is no short-cut to Flaubert's successful formula. Some beginning writing students say they want to write poetry, but they don't want to read any. That's uncool. It's an approach that will almost guarantee bad writing, or, at the least, ignorant writing. That sense of *the right world in the right place every time* cannot wholly be instilled from without. It must also come from deep reading—from a deep communion with the printed page. "Surround yourself with good sentences," Jane Kenyon instructs.

The only way to approach Flaubert's formula is: practice the craft.

To take an example from the visual arts: A fortunate stroke of paint appears on the canvas, out of nowhere. Well, not out of *nowhere*. It has been long prepared for; or the artist has long prepared to recognize its worth. Talent makes for good luck. Craft is required for the fortunate accident to happen. In this way the artist surprises, and is surprised. Long preparation makes for readiness. A painter-friend of mine was asked at a recent show, "How long did it take you to paint this painting?" She answered, "All my life."

One of my favorite cartoons from the *New Yorker* showed a doctor and a writer at a cocktail party. The doctor says, "When I retire from surgery, I'm going to write a novel." And the writer replies, "When I retire from writing, I'm going to be a surgeon."

Information

My brother is a poet. He writes these wonderful haikus that come with long discursive footnotes. Sometimes the footnotes go on for pages. There is a lot of poetry in his footnotes, as well as information.

The other day, my brother and I were sitting around talking about all the information we possess that seems useless, except maybe for putting into poems, or footnotes.

"When God invented language," my brother said, "there was already a word for it in Sanskrit."

"Crossing rivers can bring disaster," I said.

My brother opened a beer. "In ancient Egypt," he said, "women made water by standing up, men by sitting down."

"I did not know that," I said, "but I do know that blood is magnetic, and that redheads are often left-handed."

"Do you know," he said, pausing to take a long swig of his beer, "that radish and radical share the same linguistic root, but that its meaning is unclear?"

He had whetted my thirst. I got myself a beer, and our talk turned to the subject of our deceased father, one of the great mysteries of our lives.

"Do you remember," I said, "our father worked the *New York Times* crossword puzzle in ink, and if he made a mistake he lost, which means he worked it all out in his head?"

"Our father drank only expensive German beer," my brother said, "from a stein inscribed with the Latin for *Don't let the bastards get you down.*"

"Our father got through medical school on his photographic memory."

"Yes," my brother added, "and he never forgot a grudge, either."

"We were vacationing in Nassau," I recalled, "and our luggage got lost, and since we were still wearing our traveling clothes they seated us behind a pillar next to the kitchen door in the dining room of our hotel, and in a snit our father sent back his steak and refused to eat anything else."

"Do you remember that car place?" my brother asked. "Sam Swope's Automobiles, and their slogan, '*Nobody walks away.*'"

"Yes, and our father was proud of saying that *he* walked away."

"He was the only one."

My brother and I lapsed into a companionable silence. After a while, he said, "Of course, all these things happened in his waking life."

I concurred.

"In his other life," my brother said, "we have no idea what he did."

One Writer's Beginnings

My grandmother's house in Old Louisville, where I lived as a child, had a small backyard that sloped abruptly to a brick alley. Her garage was dug into the hill, its flat roof only a step up from the yard, and the front lip of that roof made a wonderful vantage point—a dreamy spot to lie on my stomach and look out over the maze of little streets and houses teeming with children and cats and delivery trucks and laundry snapping in the magnolia-scented breeze.

The house across the alley held many mysteries. Nary an adult came or went. An army of children played or squabbled in the dirt yard among a scruffy menagerie of dogs and chickens. I lay on my garage roof, my chin on my arms, and tried to imagine their inner lives, inside that clapboard house, inside their tousled heads. This enchanted watching, I suppose, began my education as a writer.

Sometimes today, when I drive downtown, I detour through that alley. The house and garage are still there, and I glance up as I drive past to see if perhaps there is some new boy up on that roof, watching me.

I count it a lucky accident to have grown up in my grandmother's house. My own mother became the *doyenne* of the household, a gravitational star among the great-aunts and female cousins. And, for a time, I existed as the only child in this small community of women. It was a sort of pediatric harem.

The men of our family were all dead or gone. Gone to find their fortunes, or their reward. I did not notice their absence until much later on. "Men come and go," an aunt remarked once, "women are the place." She made that remark in the kitchen, and I can remember how it hung in the air, like a sharp aroma. Even now I can call it to mind: cinnamon, burnt.

My grandmother and her sister, whom she affectionately called "Sister," were well-mated for widowhood. One pieced, the other quilted. One washed, the other dried. One did windows, the other floors. It was a house of working women, make no mistake— washing, darning, ironing, sweeping, waxing, airing, cooking.... Mattie and Iley were farm women, only recently moved from Owen County to the city. They lived out-of-doors as much as possible. They kept chickens in the back yard, and Iley, big as she was, could move like the wind and chase down a chicken and break its neck with a snap of her fingers.

Iley's style of cookery was creative and chaotic. She proceeded with dashes of this and handfuls of that, moving amid clouds of flour dust, bubbling grease, whistling steam. There was always a great clanging of pots and pans, and she sang along, or loudly hummed. Long strands of her frizzy gray hair strayed from her hairnet. In the building heat, her pale face flushed, and an aura, or halo, seemed to form about the soft contours of her ample body, signifying a source of unearthly energy just when she might have needed it most.

To my young mind, she seemed more a conjurer than a cook. For, out of the whirlwind of the kitchen would come a splendid procession of dishes: bowls of green beans with ham and onions;

bowls of mashed potatoes churned with butter, sweet milk and pepper; small tureens of thick brown gravy; bowls of greens still smelling of the earth, and spiced with vinegar and garlic; baskets of toasty, cigar-shaped cornbreads; platters of friend chicken and corn-on-the-cob.

At every Sunday dinner, in the middle of the table, there floated a single magnolia blossom, cut from the tree in our front yard, in a bowl of water. Its perfume, layered between the chicken and the kale, is still what Sundays smell like. I have only to pass a blooming magnolia tree and am transported back to #11 Innis Court, with its wide front porch, the glider looking across the street to the broad flat lawn of the old folks home, and long afternoons idled away in anticipation of the dinner hour.

My job, as a boy, was to roam the length and breadth of our little *cul-de-sac*, and to wear myself out with wonder.

No other children lived on our street. Only war widows, nuns, and a few old men. So I found my fellow creatures in the sprites that lived in the limestone walls, and in the spirits of the elephant trees on the broad Altenheim lawn, and in the animus of the clouds in our little patch of sky. Although my world lay bound to that one short street, my legs found no end of places to go.

At night, cross-eyed weary, I dropped into my narrow bunk and was lulled to sleep by the lowing of the far Butchertown trains; the soft revolution of car-light on the ceiling; those magnolia-scented breezes. I dreamed deep and well-nourished dreams, floating along the rivers of Babylon, where all of life's wonders fill the night sky with loud and terrifying colors, and where a boy's hopes and fears are daubed on the bright blue dome of the mind.

With Ginsberg

I'm with you in Rockland,
where you must feel very strange
(from "Howl")

When Allen Ginsberg came to visit my class, I tried to prepare my students for the experience by telling them about the famous Gallery Six reading, when the world first heard his poem "Howl." I told them about the Beat Hotel in Tangier, and hippies, and the early days of the gay rights movement.

When Ginsberg showed up, at my classroom door, wearing a banker's gray three-piece pinstripe suit and tie, and fussing with a satchel of papers, I think my students were momentarily disappointed.

Once he collected himself, though, he led off with a couple of exercises—word games—to loosen us up. "Love consonants," he cooed, "but savor vowels."

Then he had us all write a little poem, and this is how we did it: He asked us to choose a word, a concrete noun, to begin with. "Make a list of concrete nouns," he said, "then choose the best one." (From my list, I chose the word "saxophone.") Now, he said, find a word, another concrete noun, that is the first word's opposite. Not so simple as cloud/rock—something more subtle,

37

more evocative, or provocative. (I made a list, and as my best opposite to "saxophone," I chose "jello.") The students followed along pretty well. I do not remember any of their opposites, but I remember well Ginsberg's own best—Nazi milk.

Some of us went out to lunch afterwards. Ginsberg was suffering from diabetes, among other health ailments—well, he was getting on in years—and he had gone on a macrobiotic diet. We found a health-food restaurant, the Twice-Told Coffeeshop (originally a second-hand bookstore), and settled in at a large table in the back room. Ginsberg was soft spoken and often funny. He was warm with the students. He spent most of the lunch signing their copies of his books.

When Ginsberg signed a book, he didn't just sign his name; he inscribed it, and then, when he had the time, he added nifty pen-and-ink drawings on the title page or frontis-piece—cityscapes of tall buildings, with little alien ships aloft, stars and moons, and cosmic suns rising up from the ground, encircled with bursts of light and rotating auras. So, one came away with not so much a signed Ginsberg as with an illustrated Ginsberg!

There is a story about the visit Ginsberg paid to E. M. Forster's rooms, at Cambridge. It was a pilgrimage, of sorts, I imagine, to the great man, author of *Howard's End* and *Room with a View*, which, among other things, ennobled homoerotic literature in an otherwise repressive age. But Forster was not in. So Ginsberg took out his colored chalks and proceeded to illustrate Forster's door with a giant cosmic eye-ball, lightning bolts and spirit signs. Imagine the great man's surprise on returning to his rooms! It was, I think, a form of love returned, as in Ginsberg's poem by that name—

Love returned with smiles
three thousand miles
to keep a year's promise
anonymous, honest
studious, beauteous
learned and childlike
earnest and mild like
a student of truth,
a serious youth.

That poem appears in Ginsberg's book *Plutonian Ode* (my copy of which he illustrated in his cosmic sci-fi manner). On the day he completed his poem "Plutonian Ode," he and several friends conducted a meditative sit-in on the railroad tracks outside the Rockwell Corporation Nuclear Facility's plutonium bomb trigger factory in Colorado, momentarily halting a train load of waste fissile material.

Love returned, indeed!

Milosz & Heroic Poetry

In a famous incident during the recent Balkan wars, an old man carried a chair and a cello into the Sarajevo street known as Sniper's Alley. He sat down, arranged his limbs around the instrument, and began to play Albinoni's "Adagio in G." For the next eight minutes or so, no shots were fired. The war came to a halt.

The old man finished the adagio and escaped back into the city unharmed. No one shot him, or his instrument—an instrument of peace, not war. His music had enacted a cease-fire, however brief.

To be sure, the war picked up again, right where it left off.

If something within me wants to dispute Seamus Heaney's observation, "No lyric has ever stopped a tank," I cannot demur much more than to acknowledge, no lyric has ever stopped a tank *for very long*.

And yet, and yet. . . .

Czeslaw Milosz asks, "What is poetry which does not save nations or people?"

During World War II, Milosz worked with the Polish underground, and he later championed such poets as Anna Swir, who joined in the Warsaw uprising against the Nazis, in 1944, building barricades in the streets and nursing the wounded. In some ways, Milosz shares more with the soldier-poets—such as Yehuda Amichai and René Char (who worked in the French

Resistance under the *nom-de-guerre* Capitaine Alexandre)—than he does with philosopher-poets.

He relates, in *The Witness of Poetry*, a conversation he had with a member of the Communist underground, in Warsaw, under the German occupation. Milosz was expressing his reluctance at having to chose between the Nazi system and the Soviet system; he found Stalin's terror machine as reprehensible as Hitler's, and he disliked philosophically the either/or mentality. The Communard only shrugged, and said, "A million people more, a million less, what's the difference?" Milosz was aghast.

Poetry opposes itself to such cruel thought. In its mistrust of power, and yes, even language, it preserves a sense of hope. Poetry is a way of taking action. In one poem, Milosz wrote,

> *Human reason is beautiful and invincible.*
> *No bars, no barbed wire, no pulping of books,*
> *No sentence of banishment can prevail against it.*
> *It puts what should be above things are they are.*
> *It does not know Jew from Greek nor slave from master.*

In an essay for the *New York Times*, Seamus Heaney wrote, of these lines, "It is thrilling to hear the ideal possibilities of human life stated so unambiguously and unrepentantly. For a moment, the dirty slate of history seems to have been wiped clean. The lines return us to the bliss of beginnings. They tempt us to credit all over again liberations promised by the Enlightenment and harmonies envisaged by the scholastics, to believe that the deep well of religious and humanist value may still be unpolluted."

Milosz was skeptical of peace movements, and even of utopian moral action. Nonetheless, Milosz's purpose in writing, as he put it in a 1962 letter to Thomas Merton, was "a blind urge and with a hope I could be useful to some people if I succeed." Even though, at the moment of writing, it might have felt like "only gropings."

In anticipation of Czeslaw Milosz's visit to our campus, I stocked my freezer with some good Polish vodka. Milosz came, and read, and at the party following his reading, only he and the academic dean had the constitution to imbibe. The next day, driving him to the airport, I asked whether the vodka would be harmed if I removed it from my freezer, which space I needed for more comestible fare. He fixed me with his wise gaze, and in that deep accent of his, he grumbled, "Vodka's indestructible."

Perhaps that's why vodka is the drink of choice in the troubled nations of eastern Europe—its imbibed, its conferred indestructibility.

Writing in Restaurants

The playwright David Mamet recently wrote a most enjoyable book of essays and occasional pieces, called *Writing in Restaurants*, much of which he wrote in restaurants. He was likely not alone. Walk into any restaurant, coffee-shop, bar, and you're likely to see any number of people writing.

While this writer sometimes needs absolute quiet, at other times I seek out the public solitude of a small table at a neighborhood institution, and the parade of old friends and beautiful strangers.

Sometimes the muse sits down at my table. She might appear in the form of the tattooed young man from the candy shop next door. Sometimes the old guy who sits by the door muttering to himself all day (when he gets into an argument with himself, he at least takes it outside). Sometimes the muse takes the guise of the tall beautiful woman who works at the restaurant—

> *The beautiful young woman at the tea shop*
> *poured darjeeling into my cup,*
> *and it was like drinking flowers off*
> *the mountainside. Second blush from south*
> *India, she might have said. And I?*
> *I would have believed her, of course.*
> *A warm day for October, under the slow*

tick and whirr of the ceiling fan. Long-
bodied, slim, she leaned forward
at the waist and poured these flowers into
my cup, her eyes like laughing sunrises,
her black wool stockings whispering
together. The attars of rose and
hibiscus. White shoulders and her long
dark hair upswept. If my grandfather were
alive, he'd say, She's one tall drink of water.

When writing this poem, I actually did a bit of research. (Yes, poets do research.) I looked on the large signboard in the restaurant for a description of darjeeling tea—some history, some nomenclature—and I discovered that darjeeling tea is brewed of South India tea leaves in something called a "second flush." Now, "flush" had all the wrong connotations for the quasi-romantic poem I was writing, so, in a later draft, it became "blush." (Yes, poets do research, and no, we don't always abide by it.)

And what's my old grandfather doing, poking his grizzled head into this poem just at the end? Well, things happen, Kundun.

A Writer in the World

It is a cold night in January and the heat has gone out in my apartment building—gas leaks in the basement. For a while I sought to make do with a fire in the fireplace. But mine is an old-fashioned coal-burning fireplace, too small for an ample wood fire, and nobody burns coal anymore. So I have gone to the local bar in order to read and write.

A young foursome sits at a nearby table. To them, a single person with a book, or pencil and paper, is invisible. But they are of great interest. My attention is drawn to one of the men, clearly a playboy, in jeans and a brown turtleneck, with a playboy's thick lips and habit of staring at his denim thighs when anyone but him is speaking. They all smoke, the girls relentlessly. One of the girls, a blond, switches from cigarettes to cigarillos and back again, and likes to blow her smoke at the ceiling. The other girl is a brunette, a theater major, I would suppose, from the extravagant way she occupies her chair. The second man has his back to me, and, to me, he is only shaggy brown hair in a brown sweater. At a table between us, a young mother sits with her child, who is doing homework. (Perhaps their heat has gone out, too.) The child frequently interrupts herself to talk to her mother; her mother, having no one with whom to have her own conversation, answers her daughter in affectionate but clipped tones. The mother dresses fashionably, all in black. Beyond that, her circumstance and her desires are inscrutable. Perhaps her husband is in the army, over-seas. More likely, I think, she is divorced, perhaps only a few years removed from the extravagant four-some at the other table.

My wife teaches an evening class. A little after eight, she meets me at the bar. We have taken a room at the inn next door for the night. My wife is a writer, too, a poet and essayist. This afternoon we tried to write at the big table in our apartment, but it was too cold. The fire in the living room didn't reach us. She tried writing in bed for a while, and fell asleep. She is a champion napper. She walks in flush from the cold, her cheeks a strawberry-pink. Tonight, she has talked to her students about Ayn Rand, then driven over in my Volvo. Her old SAAB never wants to start in cold weather. She pulls some books from her bag. We compare reading lists. She is reading W.G. Sebald, and Jane Kenyon, and *Letters to Jane* by Hayden Carruth. I am reading Natalie Ginzburg's essays, *The Little Virtues*, and the new novel by Toni Morrison. But first we kiss.

Just a few weeks ago, we could sit in the front room and read by the golden glow of just-turned pear trees outside the French doors. The apartment is on the second floor, and so we get the full glory of the leaves' stored-up light. And now, suddenly, the leaves are all gone and a gray winter has settled in. The tree branches are a black-gray, hoar-frost covers the ground, and low clouds of a battleship-gray go scudding across the sky, as if we live in a vague military drama. We long for the stars, for a glimpse of the moon. Every hour the bells of St. James clang aloud, drilling their holy duty into the stillness of the apartment. Plus the three extra-hourly calls to mass each day. In winter, with the windows and the storm-windows closed, we often go days without hearing, or being aware of hearing, the bells. Summertime, however, the bells wake us at seven, even on Saturdays, and on Sundays they're an absolute riot of noise.

At the inn, our suite has an English hunting theme, with framed prints of riders on horseback jumping hedges, "shewing the way." And a sheep theme. And a chintz theme. It's all a little overwhelming. There is no place for the eye to rest. But it's warm. One room is a small kitchen, with an armchair, which I immediately think can be drawn up to the stove in the event of truly cold weather. The other room has a high bed behind a love-seat and console television. And sheep. And images of fox-hunting. We climb onto the bed and turn on a ballgame. We are both basketball fans. We are news junkies, too. But ever since our current president has been in office, we cannot bear to watch the evening news on television. It always breaks our hearts. We need the distance of print for the grim doings of his office in the world.

The one window in our suite, covered by a Roman shade, looks out over the parking lot of the restaurant. The inn, carved out of an old row of shops, feels claustrophobic. Such a different feeling from our large (if cold) apartment, with its eighteen windows and seventeen doors. Nonetheless, our's is a nice problem to have. In just the last fortnight, there have been tsunamis in Asia, an avalanche in the Rockies, floods in the northeast—all combined, hundreds of thousands dead. And I cannot help but think, in view of such natural disasters, war—a human invention—is gratuitous and grotesque.

We take our pleasure in quotidian joys. Conversations with students. A pleasant meal. Some good sentences written. The coming rites of spring. A new year has begun, and there must be some comfort in that. I used to make resolutions, and share them with family and friends. Now, if I make them, I make them to myself only, for I am less interested in making my failures public anymore. One of my deepest pleasures is to read, and then to look up into space, into the middle distance of my apartment, and follow out some tangent of thought, then to return to the book at hand. Sometimes these pausings more resemble the absence of thought, a blank staring at the mantelpiece, or out the window, so that what I have just read may sink in? I don't know.

The poet Wislawa Symborska has praised those three little words, *I don't know*. When tyrants and demagogues *know*, they do not listen and people suffer as a consequence. To learn something new would be contrary or inconvenient to their programs, their pogroms. To *know* is anti-intellectual. To say *I don't know* is to learn. And when is one ever finished knowing? Writers understand this at least as well as others. I am thinking, now, of another poet, the Russian Joseph Brodsky, and what he said on this subject: "If you are in banking or if you fly an aircraft, you know that after you gain a substantial amount of expertise you are more or less guaranteed a profit or a safe landing. Whereas in the business of writing what one accumulates is not expertise but uncertainties. Which is but another name for craft."

The next day we have heat, and can return to our apartment. It is a pleasure to have the place restored to us. There, the large blue nude over the fireplace. There, the sickly *ficus* tree. There, the large table where we most often sit and read, write and look at the newspaper.

Art & Self

My father had the talent to be an artist, but he never did anything with it. And in that sentence turns the hope and disappointment of a lifetime.

He was an accomplished amateur watercolorist and illustrator. He would have been happy being an artist, or a teacher, but his father pushed him into medical school. For a while, he wanted to become a medical illustrator, but that too fell away, and he became a first-rate general practitioner.

When my father retired—and he retired on the day he turned 65—he went back to his art. But it wasn't the same. His talents, his knowledge, his interest had all dissipated, and, in his retirement, he spent as much time shooting pool, driving his sports car, and drinking beer as he did drawing.

If you asked him what he did all day, he'd say he piddled around. That phrase included his art. That's what his art had come to mean.

My mother was an artist, too, and she probably had the greater promise. In college, she majored in art and art history. And she was a beauty queen—Miss Thoroughbred at the University of Louisville—three years running. So, she knew a thing or two about aesthetics.

She was an oil painter, a realist, with a good command of color and a draftsman's perspective. But the only time she painted in her adult life was when her marriage to my father came apart. She executed paintings of a barn, a covered bridge, and a church in a wooded glen, and she titled them "Therapy I," "Therapy II," and "Therapy III." That's what her art had come to mean.

When her health began to fail, and she moved into a nursing home, I tried to persuade her to take up painting again, not only for her own enjoyment but also to hold at bay her encroaching senility. I set up an easel by a window, laid out her paints and brushes, bought her a drop-cloth. However, she had lost her abilities. She stared at the paints and the small canvasses I had bought her with a mix of terror and uncertainty. She never made an attempt.

She pooh-poohed the "therapy paintings" that hung in her small apartment. Once she told me she could not believe she had ever painted them, "bad as they are."

I was in my mid-forties, and comfortable in a routine of teaching at a small college and writing poems, when I began to think about my parents' talents, and the loss of those talents. I also began to think about my own place in the queue and whether I was coasting, piddling, going intellectually senile.

So I rented a small studio, bought paints and canvasses, and got to work, unschooled except by years of long looking at paintings, many wonderful conversations with artist-friends, and a hoped-for inherited ability. I failed, day after day. But I kept going back to it. Eventually, some little thing would go right, usually a mistake that I rather liked. I began to work *for* mistakes. I liked them because they were the least my own, and because they surprised and interested me.

After a year, I had a gallery show, and have had several shows since. But what I came to miss—*for* my parents—was not any commercial or critical success, rather the self-discovery in art, and the selflessness of art. My parents, as individuals, were each rather self-involved persons, although in quite different ways. My father indulged, my mother worried. The conversations were always about themselves—his new toys, her dire straits.

Art is service to an ideal that exists beyond personality, of and through the self but beyond the self, to a greater world of meaning and its interpretations. I wish that my parents could have joined in that conversation.

I wish they could have been less self-involved and more self-aware. Like all the arts, painting is a mode of personal inquiry. The painter gets schooled in the deep subject of him- or herself along the way. It is also a humbling act. It is good to be humble. Humility does terrific things for one's self-respect.

In their own way, each of my parents suffered a paralyzing form of self-deprecation—my father joked, my mother suffered. Late in life, each focused on earthly matters to the seeming exclusion of any wonderment at mystery, or spirit, or soul. This seemed a great loss, as well.

Art says what cannot be said otherwise. We have capabilities—mysterious and deep—beyond our knowing. Art addresses these, because these are also part of who we are. Call it the unconscious, or call it the soul. Why deny or ignore it? And why, thereby, think that we are less than we are? I wish that my parents could have been able to join in this conversation, too.

We are most ourselves when we are least self-conscious. We are perhaps least self-conscious when we experience a transcendent moment such as art provides, whether we are the creator or the viewer. When art presents us something truly beautiful, it also acknowledges the death of that thing—its moment in real time has been lost, *but for this image*. Its moment in imaginative or aesthetic time, however, can last forever. In our creation or absorption of the beautiful, we experience a buoyancy, a deathless moment. A loss of self that returns us, whole-hearted, to ourselves and to the mortal world.

Digressions on a Typewriter

I typed my first poems on a manual typewriter, and I liked the way the action embodied the words. Muscle and bone and sinew struck the keys, which levered the arms, which slammed home the chosen symbols.

My fingers and hands became strong. My words bit into the paper. Writing became a pleasingly physical act, like sculpting a top-spin lob. Boys are often physical learners, education experts tell us, and I believe them. Boys like to read while walking, and to carve equations into tree-trunks, and other such things.

Typing on my Smith-Corona (all gray and silver, with green racing stripes) was like playing the piano, but much better, because the musical sounds evaporated, whereas the literary sounds turned into indelible marks on bond paper. And these sounds (of mine, at least) were more pleasing to the ear.

Some peculiar facts about typewriters—

1) Why are the letters arranged as they are? So that typewriters salesmen, back in the day, could type the word TYPEWRITER musically and efficiently, using only the top row of keys, in demonstrations.

2) The composer Antonin Dvorak's cousin, I think it was, invented a typewriter keyboard that equalized the

work between the right and left hands, but it never caught on. Why does the left hand do most of the work?

3) Janis Joplin and her band in the 1960s, Big Brother and the Holding Company, sometimes used typewriters as percussion instruments. The German composer Moritz Eggert wrote a symphony for manual typewriters, most recently performed at the Canadian International Sound Symposium.

When I was in college, we all typed our papers on typewriters. (The personal computer had not been invented yet.) We fussed with ribbons, white-out, onion-skin paper, colas and occasionally other stimulants. The clatter of old machines echoed up and down the halls.

If we found a mistake in a paper, we had to type the offending page over again, making sure to end on the same word at the bottom, lest we have to re-type the next page also. We strove for content—to reach the assigned page length—even though the muscles in our hands ached.

With poetry, it was different. We strove for conciseness, precisely because every word came with its physical price. And any word or phrase that bored the author got omitted. They say (they say!) that writers working at computers write more, because the typing is easier. Not better, necessarily, just more. I don't know if this is true.

I cannot compose at a computer. Born before their advent, I can think only with pencil and paper in hand. I cannot compose at a keyboard. Once a draft is fairly well in hand, I type it on my typewriter to see the exact measurements of the lines, to see the structural shape of the poem.

Crossing Fifty

On the occasion of my fiftieth birthday, some writer-friends and students gathered around a long table under a tree on the terrace of a downtown restaurant, and we drank and talked the night away. One of the writers who couldn't make it, the poet James Baker Hall, sent a note in which he said, among other things, "Fifty gets one free of youth, and its excuses and postponements."

At one end of our table sat the venerable poet, novelist, essayist Wendell Berry, whose maturity (he's into his 70's) has only made him sharper and more prolific than earlier in his writing life. At the other end of the table sat some of my current and former students, so filled with notions of the writing life, and so uncertain about their destinies as artists.

Gazing at my students, I thought about the many years I lost in my youth, making excuses and procrastinating, not knowing that's what I was doing. Thinking that I had to be this kind of poet, or that kind of poet—anything but myself. I wanted to be from New York, or Trieste. I wanted my parents to be disgraced nobility. I wanted anything but my own life. It wasn't until I dropped the pose of my disaffection that I truly began to write.

In the preface to a recent book of his own, Wendell Berry referred to himself as an "amateur" poet. He has caught the essence of the practice here, for one never masters the art, rather, one serves a life-long apprenticeship. Naturally, one gets better with age. I tell my students that their chief disadvantage is their youth, and, with time, this will be overcome.

And, Jim Hall is right, I feel. At fifty, one picks up, as a faint rustle on the horizon, time's winged chariot. Maybe it's not hurrying near, just yet. But it is beginning to agitate the air.

So, I began to imagine the ripeness of old age—

> *I grew old. Days dawned with a certainty*
> *that I envied. In the mornings I listened*
> *to jazz, barking dogs, and to the cemetery*
> *geese. I read novellas, and short poems.*
> *At noon I lunched on goat cheese and bread,*
> *then napped. I bought a copy of Aquinas,*
> *"The Summa of the Summa," the best of the best,*
> *and read a section per day—thereafter,*
> *on good days, I drank the wine of the wine,*
> *and heard the birdsong of the birdsong.*
> *The laurel of the laurel grew round my head.*
> *At night I went walking in the forest,*
> *and the moon that rose in the western sky*
> *was the moon of the moon.*

On Teaching

In my teaching career, I have had the good fortune of learning from many fine students. One of them was a 4th-grader. She wrote a poem from the point of view of a coconut, concluding, "I never have to go on vacation / because I carry the waves inside me."

Children are natural poets. It is important that we not teach the poetry out of them. They will not all grow up to become writers, but, whatever they do, we will need their creative problem-solving.

Mostly I teach college students, those curiously adult children. Here, too, teaching creative writing seems a matter of modeling some practices and techniques, then getting out of the way. They are so ready to become the world. And the world will be better for it.

Again, not all of my advanced students, even, will become professional writers. But, in order to lead an examined life, anyone ought to be able to write a poem—to reflect on one's life in language. Certainly that was the case in ancient China. During the Sung dynasty, candidates for civil service exams were required, among other tasks, to compose a poem on a theme presented to them at the moment. We might ask no less of our own citizens, if we wish to live in a truly enlightened democracy. I might even say one needs this ability in order to lead a good life.

Writing poetry is a gift, like a mule—if you don't work it, it's no good. But it is not hard work. Hard work is driving a truck or waitressing.

My thinking about poetry does not amount to a theory, or system, much less a philosophy. In fact, my classroom runs more like a shop class than a literature class. I tell my students that writing a poem is like building a birdhouse—you can talk all day about the aesthetics of the thing, but if no birds come to live in it, then it's not much good, is it?

Whatever they do with their lives, my students will have spent a year or two dealing in the creative possibilities of language. They will have had a couple of semesters or more to write poems—a great luxury, I tell them, in this world of hardship and repression and cultural prejudices.

At my college, the business school graduates two hundred young executives each year. The nursing school graduates a hundred nurses. The education school graduates a hundred teachers. My numbers are more modest. It pleases me to think of the college of Arts & Sciences graduating a few "culture workers" each year—people who will make art, or who will enable the making of art, for themselves and also for the young executives, nurses, teachers, shopkeepers. . . .

It only takes six hundred people to make a culture, Ezra Pound decided.

Début

A new poet débuted last night, giving a glorious reading at a club downtown. If this were Russia in the 1920's, or Paris in the 50's, or Beirut at any time in the last century, she would have come home to find flowers heaped by her front door, and the morning papers would be trumpeting her achievement.

These were the things I told her as I held her in my arms this morning. She had awakened to the world as it was before her début, when she still wrote in secret, unsure of her abilities, and unaware of the deeper truths being realized in her lines. Then, slowly, the events of last night came back to her. Her world had shifted on its axis. I watched her eyes light up. A secretive smile came into her lips.

"Ezra Pound said it only takes six hundred people to make a culture, and forty of them were there last night listening to you read your poems," I told her.

"Yes," she said. "Forty. Or fifty."

I could see her mentally counting the house.

She had been a singer (opera) in her younger days, and so she knows how to command a stage. Even younger, she had performed Shakespeare at the Folger Library. But those were other people's words. Last night, she read her own words, to an audience of the initiated, and they applauded her every poem.

These were the words she had crafted herself—afternoons curled up on the futon under the de Kooning print; evenings on the sleeping porch with a breeze coming in through the trees; mornings at her desk with its view of the neighbor's garden and his rambunctious greyhound. All these things appear in her poems, too, if not as themselves, then as sparkling particles of the warmth and grace that her poems exude.

The forty (or fifty) people in her audience last night sat in a darkened silence and she brought them figures and breezes and gardens and greyhounds, and she brought them beauty and stillness and worship.

"Your poems are still out there, floating around, part of the day's very weather," I told her.

She seemed to need this reassurance. We lay in bed curled up together, listening to the birds, and, though this was not Russia or Paris or Beirut, what I said seemed to be true.

A Poet's Alphabet

A is for Anna Akhmatova, the Russian poet, with whom I share a birthday, St. John's Eve, when the spirits of the world (both good and evil) are at their strongest. As a child, Akhmatova rightly predicted that she would become a famous poet, and that an obsidian statue would be erected to her near her hometown of Odessa. She could not have foreseen that her verses would be on the lips of everyday Russian women waiting with her in the lines outside Soviet prisons, hoping to see their sons, husbands, brothers.

B is for the billowing clouds outside the classroom window. B is for breaking the rules and not listening when the teacher is talking, but staring out the window and working out the world as *you* know it. Lost in thought, the student travels far in advance of the lesson plan. Too many of our schools nowadays have been built to resemble minimum-security prisons, built, as they are, of concrete and wire, with no accessible windows, and thus nowhere to look when the teacher is a bore. B is also for brilliance, achieved in moments unnoticed by the educational authorities.

C is for Certainty, of which the poet has none. Not about his talent, nor his fame, nor the truth of his verses. He has only a wish (see W) that his lines capture some ineluctable vivacity, and the certainty that he must write, however uncertain the outcome.

D is for Dutch, the language of my ancestors, which I do not speak. But I do paint in the Dutch way: ninety per-cent of my canvas is sky. Egg-shell blue, lemon orange. The sky has its own geographies, its own tumults, whilst our ephemeral lives pass underneath like the rivers endlessly flowing. The Dutch language, like many northern European tongues, is so guttural, and of the throat, and I speak so nasally, that I would need a surgical procedure to speak it properly.

E is for enjoyment. A poem is meant to provide pleasure. Of course, it's a deep pleasure that poetry gives, which is different from, say, happiness. Happiness is a skittery condition, and much foolishness is undertaken in its name. The outward sign of happiness is a big toothy grin such as you see in toothpaste ads on television. Pleasure can be registered on a human face without the hint of a smile. Its center lies deeper in the body, and is tinged with sadness, because pleasure has an end. But it is a knowing sadness, and so this gives pleasure, too. (See also O for Ovid.)

F is for free verse, which is a lot harder than it seems. Because poetry, like water, needs a container. Frost said free verse is like playing tennis with the net down. But can you imagine? That would be impossible. No, free verse is like playing tennis with the net *up*, because every poem comes with some inherent shape and, thus, limitation, but with mutable lines, perhaps, because a good poem takes us wider or deeper than we meant to go.

G is for ghazal, the Arabic form of poetry. An intimate form of address, it often works in couplets, with a repeating phrase and a repeating rhyme. It is a good poetic form for reciting aloud in taverns and coffeehouses, from Beirut to Riyadh to Dayton. I ask my students to write ghazals and to chant them aloud to the class, so that they can become a little bit Arabic. So that they may be able to see a little further than gun-sights or the television evening news will allow.

H is for Hot Rod Hundley. Every high school has one, and he has given us a life-time of stories, in just four short years, to tell and re-tell in our poems. The time he drove his motorcycle through the halls. The time he unfurled a Vietnamese flag at a pep rally. The way he used to fold aluminum foil gum wrappers into thin strips, slide them into an electrical outlet, then toss paper-wads at them till they touched and blew out the lights. We know now about multiple intelligences; Hot Rod Hundley had a genius for trouble. He would never write a poem himself. He hated poetry. But he *was* a poem.

I is for the I of the poem, which is not the author, of course, but the speaker, a wholly invented creature who nonetheless takes the heat for the author. The I in a poem declaims, proclaims, exclaims, but does not claim any relation to the person behind the curtain. This I is often a renegade, going off and doing things the author is too timid to consider. Like a Walter Mitty character. Or, better yet, the dual roles played by Jerry Lewis in "The Nutty Professor"—the nerd and his chemically-induced alter-ego, the rake.

J is for juvenilia, a shameful though necessary part of every poet's *ouevre*. Most poets begin writing early, and our early works are not for public consumption. However, in the first flush of composition, we think these new works magnificent. We show them to people, who may act enthused, but even before the looks of approval have faded from their eyes, our cheeks are beginning to burn with the shame of what we have just written. Already, in the second flush of composition, the juvenile poem begins to betray us, with trite phrasings and bad rhymes and silly ideas that only now (too late) become apparent to us. Juvenalia is what gets hidden away, and perhaps rightly so.

K is for the public gardens of Kyoto, for no other reason than that they do not need to exist, and yet they do. As such, K is for all things that do not need to be, and yet are, like kites, and trilby hats, platypuses and kiwis. They enlarge our world and, more importantly, our imaginations, by freeing them both from the rigors of logic and necessity.

L is for Louisville, my home town, birthplace also of boxer Muhammad Ali. To have grown up in Louisville when Ali boxed in his prime is to have lived and died with his every fight. When he won, euphoria swept the streets; when he lost, the city sat slumped in a corner, a towel over its head. My father worked as Ali's ringside doctor in his amateur days, and I tagged along, and I remember the honey-brown skin of his large hand enveloping my fist in a handshake. He was big and brash and every boy in Louisville wanted some of that. Ali was always complicated, often paradoxical. How many other boxers composed a poem before every fight? *Float like a butterfly, / sting like a bee.* Ali was at once a brutal scientist and a man of peace. He once won a match without throwing a punch. Sparring with then-champion Ingemar Johanssen, in 1960, Ali slipped every punch the champ threw, for two rounds, without raising his hands from his side, and at last the champ's trainer stopped the fight, afraid the champ would throw out his back. Non-violent boxing! A kind of poetry, I think.

M is for Osip Mandelstam, who got into trouble with Stalin when he compared the dictator's thick mustache to a pair of cockroaches on his upper lip. For that he was sent to Siberia. A story came out of the prison camp there, that Mandelstam had been invited to a thieves' den to recite his poems. He went, and he recited his poems by candlelight, and none of the thieves stirred except to offer him bits of torn black bread, or to ask him to repeat a verse—

> In the northern capital
> a dusty silver poplar pines away;
> caught in its leaves,
> a clock's transparent dial....

And the thieves, looking at the poet in their midst, saw the crenellated towers of the capital city. And they saw, in a dark square, the silver poplar grown straight and tall. And through its leafy carriage, they saw the moon-like clock, whose hands moved slowly, or not at all.

N is for noise and its opposite, silence, which a poet needs. The lonely silence of a hotel room on the inside of a building well. The ecstatic silence of a mountaintop. The silence of a dawn drive through the bluegrass before the grooms have awakened the horses. N, then, is a negative category. The poet often deals in negation itself. Call it "the shadow life," or "the life not lived." This pertains to the realm of the possible, otherwise known as hope. Pleasant noise does exist, like human conversation, trams in the distance, the singing of children, and, on any beach, *bossa nova* music.

O is for Ovid, of course, whose verses titillated the aristocracy until he fell out of favor with the emperor and was exiled to Romania, the Italianate version of Siberia. Ovid was a poet of pleasure, which is what got him into trouble. His *Art of Love* offended Caesar Augustus (who was all about the Roman version of family values). Ovid never wrote of pleasure that he did not also foresee its end, which only made the pleasure more intense. His famous Fifth Elegy, about a summer afternoon's assignation with the lovely Corinna—"I cling'd her naked body, down she fell," in Christopher Marlowe's translation—ends not with the poet sated, but with his longing for more—"being tired she bade me kiss, / Jove send me more such afternoons as this."

P is for palimpsest, one of my favorite words. A palimpsest is a word, or canvas, or any surface, really, through which previous surfaces show, achieving some aesthetic effect. As Nabokov put it in his novel *Transparent Things*, "the past is always shining through the present." Like a thin layer of ice in which a frozen coin, or the tracks of yesterday's skaters, can be seen. The canvas, then, becomes three-dimensional, and incorporates the fourth dimension of Time, as well.

Q is for quixotic, which refers to the noble fool in us all. Or does it? What does the self-proclaimed knight errant Don Quixote—whose mind has been ruined by reading chilvaric novels—stand for? Is he a tragic hero? Or is he meant by his author to be an object of ridicule? The novel seems to leave these questions open. But that's okay, and maybe irrelevant; language is changeable, and if people want *quixotic* to mean "noble fool," then it does. It is perhaps the noble fool in me that writes poetry, i.e., tilts at windmills. (I have read Cervantes' novel twice, once recently, in English, and once long ago, in the original Spanish, and I find the novel tedious in the extreme, an endless string of jokes with always the same punch-line. But mine is not the popular reading of *Quixote,* oft by those who have never read it.)

R is for Rumi, the mystical poet of 13th century Persia. His poems celebrate both sensuality and spirituality in the most tender language. I used a poem of Rumi's as the epigraph to my third book of poems—*I saw you last night at the gathering, / but could not take you openly in my arms, / so I put my lips next to your cheek, / pretending to talk privately*—and my ex-wife thought it referred to a love affair, but I meant it to signify the privileged speech that poetry is, for both the reader and the hearer.

S is for Sappho, who is nearly anonymous. None of her poems exist in her own hand, but only as quoted in other people's writings about her. Some say she represents the first in a long line of classical women poets, but, in another sense, she represents the last in a line of pre-classical women poets, all of them long lost to us now. Whether they hailed from the island of Lesbos or else-where is no matter. In a recent biographical dictionary, the page for Sappho is left blank—the reader is invited to supply his or her own information, since so little is known of her, and since so much of that is supposition. Did she throw herself off a cliff for the love of a ferryman? Was she a lesbian? How did she know so expertly that a thin line of fire runs under the skin of the lover?

T could be for many things (Terpsichore, *terza rima*, trumpet, etc.), but here it is for trees, my companions since childhood. I have climbed their limbs and whispered my secrets to their leaves, and they have listened with the patience and wisdom of grandfathers. I still find them companionable presences, enduring and existential. Perhaps I am thinking of the elephant trees on the altenheim lawn when I was a boy, or the beech on the front lawn of the family estate, or the brace of Bartlett pear trees before my second-floor porch, home to pigeons, hard inedible fruits, and breezes from the cool north.

U is for the unusual, the unexpected. In this sense, U is a negative category, but not like N, because U posits something positive—an alternative way of seeing or perceiving. U is not negation. U is affirmation of the underside. U is the way things would be otherwise, and how often do we long for that?

V is for Vivaldi, especially his *Four Seasons* suite. I often listen to classical music when writing. There is something both bright and soulful in Vivaldi's music. For me, it is best played in the early afternoon. Bach's *Double Violin Concerto* is best first thing in the morning, especially that sweet second movement. Followed, later in the morning, by the delicate plinkings of Satie, which I sometimes sit down and pick out on the keyboard to my own slower pace. Late afternoon is for the baroque cello, early evening for Beethoven's piano sonatas. Late night is for silence, the stars sparkling overhead and the west winds soughing through Respighi's pines.

W is for wish, which the poet expresses every time he sits down to write. Of course, to write poetry is to practice an ancient craft, like water-divination, for which the modern world might seem to profess no use. But do not be fooled. There is as much need for clean water and poetry now as ever. In fact, if we focused more on basic needs and less on superfluous distractions, clean water and poetry would be near the top of anyone's list. The critic Helen Vendler recently called for politicians to study history less—we seemed doomed to repeat history, she said, no matter how well we know it—and to consider poetry more. Consult Dante, not Machiavelli. We will profit more by the poets.

X is for Xavier Cugat, the big-band leader, for the music of his name. Other favorite names of mine, because they are just so much fun to say aloud, include the tennis player Gabriela Sabatini, mezzo-soprano Frederica von Stade, basketball players Dikembe Mutumbo and Tayshaun McBroom, football player I. M. Hipp, skater Oksana Baiul, and writers Chinua Achebe, F. Scott Fitzgerald, Jhumpa Lahiri, and, of course, Gabriel Garcia Márquez.

Y is for yes. "No" requires explanation. "Yes" is a simple affirmative, and requires none. The poet—even in the harshest of times—says, "Yes." And it resounds in the darkest corner of the world.

Z is for zyzzyva, the last word in the dictionary (meaning a kind of boll weevil), also, a literary journal published on the west coast by my friend Howard Junker. Such journals, and the small press generally, in this country, discover the new talent; this is where the national literature gets created. When I edited a literary journal, *The American Voice*, the most exciting part of every day was collecting the mail—what wonderful surprises awaited me there? What marvelous discoveries? As a writer, now, I still live by the postman's ring. I am a mail slut. And I am nostalgic for the time, earlier in the last century, and quite before my time, when mail came at least twice a day.

Letter from Paris

Tonight, in Paris on fall break, we have taken a small room on the top floor of a hotel just off the boulevard St-Michel. It is an odd little room. No right angles anywhere, and every wall is of a different surface, stone, brick, plaster, paper. The furniture in the room is Typical Hideous. But, the furnishings do not matter. What matters is that the room comes cheap. And that we can lie in the bed and look out over a squabble of rooftops, chimneys, antennae, sky and birds. And that I can turn the desk around into the window-niche and sit up late writing lines in my journal, looking down into the courtyard, and into the windows of my neighbors. In one, an old man sits before an easel, a dog napping at his feet. In another, shadows slow-dance behind a thin muslin curtain. For a while, light enough to write by came down from the sky. Later I burned a candle. The desk, turned round into the window-niche, which itself is cut into the mansard roof, creates a little room of its own, at the edge between interiority and exteriority. I can feel the warmth of our room at my back, and, through the open window, the cool air of the evening on my face. Within such a courtyard as this that we have found, here at the two-star Hôtel Europe St-Séverin, dozens of possible lives present themselves, framed in their own windows for viewing. On the roof-garden, a young man in a flowered housecoat waters some plants, then stoops to pick up a cat. In one corner, inside the five-storey tier of windows, a

71

circular staircase curls upward, the same graceful curve repeating floor after floor, like the refrain of a popular song. The Latin Quarter being a very old place—so old that it used to be avant-garde—aids me in my thinking. Its antiquity reminds me that everything has happened before. This comes as a reassurance. St.-Germain-des-Pres was overrun by Nazis, yet it has survived to be beautiful once again, flowers tumbling in profusion from its iron balustrades. So. An hour or two of composition. A time of deep stillness, into which the stars cast their tiny bolts of love. Then, a walk among the crowds in the streets. Dinner in a Japanese restaurant on the rue St-Séverin, with fresh flowers in a little vase on our table, and the singular flame of a white tea candle. Then, out into the crowds again, pausing to look at the dubious talents on display near the Metro—a man carving canaries out of carrots, a man putting out cigarettes on his palm—and stopping to look in the windows of bookshops. Come the morning, we will wander out into all the rain-bright colors of autumn, which arrives while we sleep. Brown crabby leaves blowing down on the sandy square of St-Sulplice, looking like Rilke's "cheap winter bonnets of Fate." Clouds bunching up on the horizon. A sharpness to the air. Should we decide to stay here, soon we should hear the church-bells only at noon.

Poetry & the Elegant Solution

Might we think of poetry in terms of the Elegant Solution? This, of course, is the phrase mathematicians give to problem-solving of the most inventive kind. It can be applied to any field of endeavor, say, when Fred Astaire ad-libs a new dance step, or when Sherlock Holmes solves a crime in some neat, unforeseeable way.

Or, to take an example from the history of mathematics, what a young German schoolboy named Carl Friedrich Gauss accomplished. (Gauss was a contemporary of Beethoven, though the two never met.) His math teacher one day gave the class the assignment of adding together all the numbers from 1 to 100, perhaps to get them to quieten down. Gauss thought for a moment, then wrote the number 5,050 on his paper. He sat patiently while his classmates slogged through the one hundred or so steps toward the answer. Those who eventually arrived at 5,050 were correct, no more or less so than Gauss. But what distinguished Gauss was *how* he solved the problem. He had suddenly perceived that adding pairs of numbers from either end of the spectrum—1 + 100, 2 + 99, 3 + 98, etc.—always produced a sum of 101. Since there are fifty pairs, the answer could be arrived at by multiplying 101 by 50.

Anyone can add up the numbers and get the correct answer. Gauss achieved the correct answer without adding up the numbers.

An elegant solution, to be sure. (Gauss went on to become a famous mathematician and astronomer, but, of his many accomplishments, he most enjoyed telling this little story about himself.)

A poem, then, can be a solution to a rhetorical problem. A good poem, an original poem, can be an elegant solution, because it expresses itself in a previously unimaginable way. A poem can turn on a sudden perception, like Gauss' solution, on a flash of insight, seemingly out of the blue. However, a poem is art, not mathematics, and therefore slippery, like spilled mercury. From the point of view of the poet, the 'problem' might not be apparent until the solution has made it so, or the poem might solve another problem than the one thought to be at hand. From the point of view of the reader, the problem is always changing over time, as the reader changes. There are other possibilities, too, perhaps as many as there are poems.

We are not thinking, here, of the poem as a mechanical solution to the stylistic demands of rhyme, meter, etc., of a sonnet or villanelle. (But this has obvious applications. A colleague of mine, Harriet Levin, teaches at Drexel University in Philadelphia, and she says her engineering students relish tackling sonnets and villanelles with all of their structural requirements.) Rather, we are thinking of the poem as a solution to the problem of meaning. Take William Carlos Williams' "The Red Wheelbarrow" as an example—

so much depends
upon

a red wheel
barrow

glazed with rain
water

beside the white
chickens

This famous little poem has been much analyzed, and most of us would accept the notion that it is, among other things, a solution to the problem of how carefully we must attend to the details of this life. Still, as Thom Gunn reminds us, we must sometimes look into the impulse behind the writing of a poem to find its meaning. So when we learn that Williams, a pediatrician, wrote that poem while sitting at the bedside of a dying child, deeper meanings open up for us. Now, additionally, the poem solves for us something on the order of love and grief.

Let us take as another example Yehuda Amichai's poem "Autumn Rain in Tel Aviv," in Chana Bloch's translation—

A proud, very beautiful woman sold me
a piece of sweet cake
across the counter. Her eyes hard, her back to the sea.
Black clouds on the horizon
forecast storm and lightning
and her body answered them from inside
her sheer dress,
still a summer dress,
like fierce dogs awakening.

That night, among friends in a closed room,
I listened to the heavy rain pelting the window
and the voice of a dead man on tape:
the reel was turning
against the direction of time.

There is much that we might expect to be told in this poem that we are pointedly not told. Who is the dead man? What is he saying? What is the relation of the speaker to the dead man? Then we realize: that is not what's being worked out here. Though we are perhaps aware of the political situation in Israel, to which Amichai obliquely refers, this poem is also about certain irresistible, terrifying, universal sensations: the turning of the seasons, the end of desire, political despair. And, of course, it is about much more.

Or consider Robert Bly's poem "What We Provide." Here, the poem is written almost as if it were an explicit solution to the problem, What is love?

Every breath taken in by the man
who loves, and the woman who loves,
goes to fill the water tank
where the spirit horses drink.

Reading the first two lines, attentive to the straightforward syntax, we might think we are going to receive one kind of a solution, a matter-of-fact response to the implied question. Ah, but we do not. Instead, in those last two lines, we receive something ethereal, dreamlike, and unforgettable because we will never quite figure it out. And is this not love? And an elegant solution thereof?

Many poems are of necessity jagged, raw, replete with harsh truths, in whose presence an aesthetic notion of "elegance" might seem politically or morally inappropriate. But we are addressing here an elegance of mentation, not of style. Form following function, the elegant solution might require an inelegant form. Consider Jan Freeman's poem "Her Oddity" —

> *Her oddity was sometimes more than she could bear.*
> *People stared at her.*
> *They wondered how she could keep it up.*
> *Her oddity often brought the melancholy out:*
> *we love you, they shined.*
> *She liked the fantasy:*
> *she played the hair and the hands,*
> *she had the wardrobe.*
> *Her oddity was deeper than a blemish.*
> *It wore her out sometimes.*

Appropriately, this is an odd poem, full of fits and starts, a fragment torn from whole cloth, deeply revealing. But this poem cannot have been written any other way. A poem can be anything so long as that anything is what it must be. This poem delivers itself up to us so completely in so few lines, we can only marvel at the elegance of its frugal accomplishment. Its oddity.

Art often succeeds according to the nature of its oddity.

The same might be said of science.

"An elegantly executed proof is a poem," says mathematician Morris Kline, "in all but the form in which it is written."

Ultimately, of course, poetry must defy our thinking of it in terms of the elegant solution. This is not so that our hypothesis (if

77

that's what it is) might be proven by its exceptions. Rather, it is simply in poetry's nature to defy explanation. And then, we will move on to think of poetry in terms of tennis, say, or the recovered palace at Byzantium.

Pax Intrantibus

The night artillery range at Fort Knox was one of the familiar sounds of my childhood. Except, for the longest time, I did not know what those soft plosive thuds might be. Lying on my bed at night, with my window propped open to the sounds of traffic on Barret Avenue, the bells of St. Therese tolling the quarter-hours, dogs barking blocks away—underneath it all, came the soft thuddings of something I could not identify. They dropped in among the other sounds of the night, as soft as commas, punctuating the darkness.

Thirty miles away, lying on his cot at the abbey of Gethsemani, the Trappist monk Thomas Merton was listening to the same sounds, and he knew full well what they were. He wrote about them in his poem "The Guns of Fort Knox"—

> Guns at the camp (I hear them suddenly)
> Guns make the little houses jump. I feel
> Explosions in my feet, through boards.
> Wars work under the floor. Wars
> Dance in the foundations.

The subterranean, hellish aspect of these shells falling is no mere conceit in this poem. Those sounds actually came up through the floorboards, not through the air, where one might have expected. Strong enough to wake the dead. But this would not be the right resurrection. "Let them sleep on, / O guns," he wrote, thinking not only of the dead but also, perhaps, of the living, the sleeping children, like me. That was just practice shelling we heard. Many children around the world go to sleep with the sound of real shells in their ears. They go to sleep, or do not go to sleep, knowing that the guns are aimed at them, and the shells are real. I was lucky. But the shells that I heard, that Merton heard, are an allegory of the real violence that exists in so much of the world.

The casual visitor to Merton's hermitage at Gethsemani can come away, after even a brief spell, with a feeling of serenity. Meditating at his hearth, browsing at his bookshelves, walking barefoot up and down in the soft pine needles.... But Merton was not about serenity. His search for peace—personal, political, spiritual—pushed him to the ends of the earth. His interior life careened between restlessness and paradox: He was a voluble man who observed monastic silence. He was a lover of women who took a vow of chastity. He was a best-selling author who renounced worldly goods.

He came to believe that a monk in the twentieth-century cannot wall himself off from the world. The Vatican tried to silence him. He tried to silence himself. But he could not keep silent. Despite his hermit ways, he became a prominent voice of dissent in a power-mad nation. He became, almost against his will, a poet-monk of social and political engagement. He openly deplored the mentality of the Cold War—the Russians did not need to build so many bombs, he said, we Americans are busy destroying ourselves—and he loudly criticized the undeclared U.S. war in Vietnam.

Like the desert fathers, those fourth-century Christian ascetics, Merton felt he had the duty to pull the world to safety.

Merton concluded that the cause of all wars is sin. And because we all bear a responsibility for the world, through grace, he blamed himself no less than Hitler for World War Two. Merton complained in his journal about this "disgusting century: the century of poison gas and atomic bombs," and then he went off to join a monastery— not to escape from the world and its problems, but to join it to God through prayerful intercession.

Merton's poem about the Nazi death camps, "Chant to Be Used in Processions Around a Site with Furnaces," refuses to allow any of us to escape responsibility for the world. The poem is written in first person, so that even the casual reader becomes the speaker, the commandant of the camp—

> *I was the commander I made improvements and*
> *installed a guaranteed system taking account of hu-*
> *man weakness I purified and I remained decent*

Stylistically, the poem abandons lyrical shape for undifferentiated blocks of prose. Thematically, Merton implicates not only the Nazis; we are all part of that deadly circle, which widens treacherously over time. Notice how eerily he anticipates the clinical warfare of such attacks as the computer-guided U.S. war against Iraq, and how he refuses to allow any of us absolution—

> *Do not think yourself better because you burn up*
> *friends and enemies with long-range missiles with-*
> *out ever seeing what you have done*

Upon learning that comic Lenny Bruce performed "Chant" in his nightclub act, Merton said, "People like Lenny Bruce are really monks in reverse."

In the poem "At This Precise Moment of History," Merton writes, "We are testing supersonic engines / To keep God safe in the cherry tree," and do we not see this happening even now in the U.S., as I am writing, as you are reading? (It is sad even that I have such confidence in asking that question.) Merton also evidences a brave ecumenism, itself prophetic, though we, here in the new 21st century, have yet to enact it. Of the Muslims in the Maldives, he writes—

> *These natives wear no pants*
> *Only aprons*
> *Bathe twice a day*
> *Use sandalwood and do not fight*
> *Their armor is prayer*

Merton's poetical argument against war goes deeper than a mere protest against violence. He understood that war-mongering attitudes proceed from grave moral and ethical illness; they are a kind of insanity of the soul. "What concerns me, perhaps this is pride, is the ghastly feeling that we are all on the brink of a spiritual defection and betrayal of Christ," he had written, in a 1961 letter to Josiah Chatham, "which would consist in the complete acceptance of the values and decisions of the callous men of war who think only in terms of megacorpses and megatons, and have not the slightest thought for man, the image of God."

And he worried about his own participation in that sort of misguided thinking. His grandfather had left him an inheritance that included stocks in heavy industry, but the young Merton scarcely tapped it. "Wherever you have oil tanks or factories or railroads or any of the comforts of home and manifestations of progress in this country, you are sure to get bombers, sooner or later," he wrote in his journal. Imagine his relief, upon signing over his inheritance to Gethsemani when he walked through its doors! Over the gates, of course, the inscription *Pax Intrantibus*: Peace Everlasting. "I am scared," he continued, in that same entry, "to own anything, even a name, let alone a coin or shares in oil, the munitions, the airplane factories. I am scared to take a proprietary interest in anything for fear that my love of what I own may be killing somebody somewhere."

Why is warfare wrong? I think Merton might have said:

Man is made in the image of God; thus, killing man kills God. A monk practices humility. Humility means trying not to offend God. Warfare is wrong because it offends God.

Poetry & Exile

A few years ago, the Hungarian-born painter known simply as Batuz founded the Societe Imaginaire. The society has no headquarters, no dues, no rules of order. But it does have nearly 500 members—writers, artists, scholars—from around the world, including the American poet Mark Strand, Mexico's Nobel laureate Octavio Paz, and Czech novelist Ivan Klima. They come together occasionally to drink and dine, talk and share ideas.

Artists from the old Eastern bloc nations see such communion as a triumph of creative will over politics. Western writers, who have enjoyed greater civil and artistic liberties, must bridge a growing cultural isolation spawned by the mass media and corporate culture.

Writers and artists do inhabit a kind of imaginary society. As Batuz explained, a poet has more in common with another poet, in another part of the world, than he has with his actual neighbor. By reading each other's work, and through correspondence, an intellectual community is formed that overcomes geographical barriers.

The imaginary society of which I am speaking reaches even beyond the grave, for is it not in his or her works that a writer achieves earthly immortality? Writers long departed still speak intimately to us, and we to them. Thus, I am describing a community of spirit.

I am also describing certain conditions of earthly exile, which seems, in the 20th century, to define the Russian poet above all, whether forced to live abroad, like Joseph Brodsky, or forcibly withheld, like Pasternak and Mandelstam; whether made a prisoner of the state, like Akhmatova, or made a prisoner of her own heart, like Tsvestaeva.

Today, we have the case of Regina Derieva. A Russian Jew by birth, she converted to Roman Catholicism and emigrated, in 1991, to Israel. However, Israel's Law of Return, which governs the right of Jews to settle in Israel, specifically excludes Jews who have chosen another faith.

For several years after her emigration, Derieva, her husband Alexander and their son lived in a state, not of exile, *per se*, but of limbo. The Soviet Union collapsed in the interim, so they could not be deported. Kazakstan, where they had lived, would not re-admit them because they are not ethnic Kazaks. For a time, they lived in an Arab suburb of Jerusalem. As of this writing, Regina, Alexander and their son are living in Sweden, while they wait for their status to be decided.

If, upon arriving in Israel, Derieva had simply declared herself a nonbeliever, she would have been allowed (under the Law of Return) to stay. Or, had she remained Jewish, and received Israeli citizenship, she then would have been free to convert to Catholicism. But, Derieva said in an interview with the *New York Times*, "I thought it was shameful to hide my faith. It was the only important choice I ever made."

In the old Soviet Union, Derieva's poetry had earned her the disapproval of the state authorities, and she was denied publication. The KGB kept close tabs on her, and she was accepted into the Union of Writers only upon the advent of glasnost. Derieva's work managed nonetheless to attract the attention of Joseph Brodsky, who first encouraged her to leave the USSR.

In her first book, *In Commemoration of Monuments*, Derieva wrote, obliquely, of her political situation, and of her spiritual circumstance as well. We recognize, in both occasions, the poetry of exile—

> *And in the wall*
> *you will find a door*
> *and in the heart*
> *and in the tree*
> *and in the heavens...*
> *Everywhere lots of doors*
> *which you cannot open*

Yet, do not poets of exile also live by hope? Derieva's second book, *Instructions for Silence*, seems to be a kind of answer. With this volume, she fits herself into the Catholic monastic tradition. These poems take up the idea of silence in many images— mountain, cathedral, snow, flowers, paper, cross. . . .

Silence, after all, is an acknowledgement of mystery. And mystery has its own powers of liberating the spirit into grace. Behind any door, she writes, "no paradise whatever, / yet paradise exists." How does she know this? By a simple sort of miracle—"a butterfly of snow / flies in the window."

The reader, like the poet, must take these words on faith. Readers too form an invisible community—a society of the imagination that does not exist except noumenally, and yet binds them together with a firm allegiance.

Late Auden

When W. H. Auden emigrated to America, in 1939, he had already written the poems that would make him famous. He settled into a Manhattan hotel room with Christopher Isherwood and began to live the life of a literary lion—fêted by Park Avenue patronesses, paid sumptuously for lectures and reviews, and tempted by the usual distractions. But he was about a serious mission—to learn to see everything through the lens of his particular gift. "One destroys one's ivory tower," he wrote, "only when one has learnt to see the whole universe as an artist, or as a scientist, or as a politician. . . ."

Whence the gift?

In an essay on Byron, Auden wrote, "The source of the poetic gift is a mystery; it is possible that, had Byron's foot been cured by modern surgery, or had his parents got on with each other, he would never have written a line. On the other hand, there are plenty of cripples and children of unhappy parents who write bad poetry or none. The study of a poet's biography or psychology or social status cannot explain why he writes well, but it can help us to understand why his poetry is of a particular kind."

What of Auden himself?

He began writing poems at the age of fifteen, elaborating, as young poets seem wont to do, a highly personal mythology.

Eventually, he would decide that "obscurity is a bad fault." Throughout the life of his career, in a great variety of forms, Auden hewed to the belief that poetry is a dialogue with its readers. Hence his famous argument with Plato, who, Auden averred, seemed unaware of what we mean by "a person." In the *Symposium*, Plato designates love of beauty as but a step toward love of an ideal. "It is quite true," Auden wrote, "that a fair principle does not get fat or run away with somebody else. On the other hand, a fair principle cannot give me a smile of welcome when I come into the room."

What of Auden's quest?

He sought out the shape of meaning. He sought to embody ideas, if possible. This bears particularly on his stature as a poet of homoerotic love. "The eternal and, probably, insoluble problem for the homosexual," he wrote, "is finding a substitute for the natural differences, anatomical and psychic, between a man and a woman."

> *I believed for years that*
> *Love was the conjunction*
> *Of two oppositions;*
> *That was all untrue. . . .*
> (1939)

Chiefly, Auden worked to reconcile poetry to politics. Yet, among the company of poets, he understood that two hundred years from now, "Nobody will care much about our politics. But if we were truly moved by the things that happened to us, they may read our poems." While he admired Rilke's visionary freedom, he also mistrusted what he saw as its indifference to human suffering. Auden was only too aware that "History opposes its grief to our

88

buoyant song." His great poem "*Musee des Beaux Arts*" argues just that point:

> *About suffering they were never wrong,*
> *Old Masters: how well they understood:*
> *Its human position; how it takes place*
> *While someone else is eating or opening a window or just*
> > *walking dully along;*
> *How, when the aged are reverently, passionately waiting*
> *For the miraculous birth, there always must be*
> *Children who did not specially want it to happen, skating*
> *On a pond at the edge of the wood:*
> *They never forgot*
> *That even the dreadful martyrdom must run its course*
> *Anyhow in a corner, some untidy spot*
> *Where the dogs go on with their doggy life and the*
> > *torturer's horse*
> *Scratches its innocent behind on a tree.*

He wrote this poem in Paris in 1938. Fascists in Italy and Germany were violently oppressing Jews, homosexuals, gypsies, and others, and the Western powers were as yet doing nothing about it, as they had done nothing against Franco's oppressions in Spain. The stanza above refers to Pieter Brueghel's painting "The Massacre of the Innocents," about Herod's attempt to kill the infant Jesus by murdering all young Jewish boys. The second stanza of this poem refers to Brueghel's "The Fall of Icarus," about the mythical boy who flew too close to the sun on wings of feathers and wax, and falls from the sky in one corner of the painting, almost unnoticed—

89

In Brueghel's Icarus, for instance: how everything
       turns away
Quite leisurely from the disaster; the ploughman may
Have heard the splash, the forsaken cry,
But for him it was not an important failure; the sun shone
As it had to on the white legs disappearing into the green
Water; and the expensive delicate ship that must have seen
Something amazing, a boy falling out of the sky,
Had somewhere to get to and sailed calmly on.

Eventually, Auden would return to Europe, and become a citizen of the world. His search for the shape of meaning would never abate. Late in life, remarking to a friend that he was looking for new influences, the friend suggested the old British poet Clough. "No, I've been through Clough," Auden replied. "I was thinking of the Beatles."

Keats, Revised

The story of Keats's life is, popularly, the story of his death. Tragically young, marvelously talented, he contracts tuberculosis while nursing his brother through the fatal disease, and dies in Rome, the eternal city, at the age of twenty-five.

Whenever this story gets told, and young Keats first coughs into his handkerchief, the savvy listener feels the chill, and longs to holler out J.D. Salinger's famous lines—

> *John Keats*
> *John Keats*
> *John*
> *Please put your scarf on.*

Keats's early life seemed destined to a dark romanticism. The son of a London stable-keeper, Keats was orphaned when still a young boy and raised by a cruel guardian, who possibly stole from the children, and who certainly considered Keats' poetic hopes ridiculous.

Later, with friends, Keats would be mysterious about his origins. He would allude to early misfortunes beyond the deaths of his parents. Perhaps he was referring to the death of his younger brother in infancy, or to other family woes. Or perhaps he was referring more sweepingly to the times. In 1795, the year of Keats' birth, Napoleon was rising out of the flames of the French Revolution and threatening to invade England. From within her green borders, England was being dangerously riven by mechanization and the revolutionary fervors of her own people. It was, as Keats would later write, "a barbarous age."

In his work, as in his life, every happiness seemed to be matched by a sorrow. His younger brother Edward died just months before the birth of his only sister. His father, after visiting the young poet at boarding school, was thrown by his horse and killed. Keats wrote, "While we're laughing, the seed of some trouble is put into the arable ground of events—while we are laughing, it sprouts, grows, and suddenly bears a poison fruit which we must pluck."

The lambent quality of his relationship to his mother especially—losing her in abandonment, recovering her, then losing her again to death—shaped a pattern of possession and loss that runs throughout his poems. He was driven by a desire to transmute absence into presence, and although he never wrote a poem directly about his parents, their loss is everywhere in his lines. Such biographical glimpses go some distance toward illuminating the strange combination of wild hope and anxiety that course through his poems. And they do help us to correct misperceptions. For example, the received idea is that Keats was some beautiful weakling, when in fact he was an indifferent student and something of a brawler!

Many of our notions about Keats had their beginnings in a fog of adoration. Shelley's elegy "Adonais" (1821) and Leigh Hunt's memoir, "Lord Byron and Some Contemporaries" (1828) both written soon after Keats' death, wrapped him up in cloaks of the rememberers' own fancies. Worse, they tended to portray him as a victim of society, of his own strivings, of a Romantic alienation.

The culture of victimhood—emotional, spiritual, alcoholic, etc.—misrepresents the artist's calling. We must remind ourselves of Keats' essential purposefulness. His early training as a doctor encouraged him to see himself as doing some good for the world, and when he gave up medicine for poetry, he saw himself as "physician to all men."

Thus he was no aloof aesthete, withdrawn and egocentric, but a poet of social and political engagement, which any careful reading of his poems will reveal. Sometimes he speaks directly, as when he castigates his countrymen for honoring the absolute monarch Charles I—"His memory, your direst, foulest shame." At other times, he speaks in allegory. Still, he struggled to reconcile a natural longing for escape with the awareness that problems cannot and should not be avoided, as in his famous "Ode to a Nightingale"—

> *Where youth grows pale and specter-thin, and dies*
> *Where but to think is to be full of sorrow*
> *And leaden-eyed despairs,*
> *Where Beauty cannot keep her lustrous eyes . . .*

It was not Keats, we should remind ourselves, who said, "Beauty is truth, truth beauty." Rather, the Grecian urn says this, in a poem criticizing a certain kind of art, "the kind from which the evils and problems of this life are deliberately excluded," as Auden put it.

Keats lived for poetry, and could not live without it. He is one of the true heroes of literature. He set himself grand themes and devoted himself to them utterly. He followed his inspiration wherever it led him—even to the army town of Newport, on the Isle of Wight, "a nest of debauchery," in Keats' view. Yet there he sojourned to write his "Endymion," a poem that would do no less than define the immortality of the human soul, and always with a sense of his own mortality. "It is just that this youngster should die away," he wrote in the preface to that poem. "A sad thought for me, if I had not some hope that while it is dwindling I may be plotting, and fitting myself for verses fit to live."

> *There is a paly flame of hope that plays*
> *Where'er I look: but yet, I'll say 'tis naught—*
> *And here I bid it die*

Going Dutch

I have been thinking about claiming citizenship in the country of my ancestors, a small non-belligerent nation in the north of Europe. True enough, Holland used to be imperial-minded. But that's behind us now. These days, we're much more into marijuana and human rights.

My father's family hailed from Utrecht, outside Amsterdam. Hendryk and Gertrude Smock came over in the 1650's and settled in the Dutch community at New Utrecht, Long Island. (They left the family coat-of-arms behind; some busy-body found it in a castle near the Rhine and sent it after them.) Hendryk and Gertrude's children and grandchildren drifted down rivers over the next three hundred years. One of them stepped off at the Ohio River portage near Louisville, and put down a few tenebrous roots.

When I trace those rivers back and return, through history, to Holland, I discover a pre-existing nostalgia in myself for beamed rooms and winding streets and canals meandering through the tall grass. My plane coming in low. Windmills and hayricks dot the fields. The flat pied landscape resembles a painter's palette, predominant greens, blues, and golds. The greatest painters have of course come from Holland, with its clean views and unsparing light. Vermeer, Rembrandt, Van Gogh. I could go on, don't need to, I feel.

Holland "paints with the right hand and writes with the left," observed the cultural historian Gerard Brom in 1939. But there seems no second-class citizenship among the modern Dutch poets, even while there is much that is painterly in their work. Lately, I have been reading up on the "rain forest-like richness," as Tonnus Oosterhoof describes it, of contemporary poetry in the Netherlands. Oosterhoof's own poems sometimes request a third art: his poem "This is where stood an apple tree" is to be read while Bach's "Inventions" plays synchronously. His poem "How gladly I saw the widower a sprig of roses" was written, he says, with the rhythms of Psalm 138 in mind:

> How gladly I saw the widower a sprig of roses
> (shears in th'other hand, he was just pruning) the lady give.
>
> I still see how the eye, the maiden's eye moist light farewell
> (by the troop-ship, by the troop-ship) had to bid farewell
> bid not had to farewell bid.
> Toot-toot. Farewell is. Pain a descending octave.
> (Each tear was one in butter ration room temperature
> Holland.)
>
> Were I to return in this flesh, the body full
> (Two, three minutes out of time, life no regret) full of
> plopper* wounds.
> I married, bred, watched tv, fire, fire, fire, fire in the
> sweet village.
> Today I lost my passport. My wife said: "Here. Take
> better care, man."
>
> Karlien van den Beukel, trans.

Is it an accident of geography—or of perception?—that much of modern Dutch poetry looks coastal? Lines lapped upon by white space, absences amongst and above the lines.... Canals divide the land itself into stanzas. And so much of the low-lying land (like the Zuider Zee) can so easily be reclaimed by silence, by the sea. There is a northern spareness here, too, perhaps in the awareness of such a marginal geographic existence. Yet we must not confuse spareness with barrenness. Terseness can reveal a great deal of emotion and information, especially in poetry. I am thinking of Elly de Waard's poems, particularly "The deep silence"—

The deep silence of a
mainland, without a coast

or line of surf, no, better
the serrated lowland on the sea

its edges thin as
postage stamps and raveled

everything there carries a watermark
or is watery; the moon

a hammered out silver disk
tear-stained behind her

97

film of mist, her veil;
the women there are sand-colored

and as blond as new wood
and just as fragrant.
                    Wanda Boeke, trans.

There came a split in post-war Dutch poetry between the more accessible, quotidian poetry of human events, on one hand, and a hermetic, spare, even impersonal poetry on the other hand. This split seems comparable to the 20th-century American separation between poets of the esoteric and the popular—Wallace Stevens, say, versus Carl Sandburg—or between those poets who sought refuge in the academy and those who still worked in the street. (This is a split in 20th-century Western thinking generally, between the hermetic and the social.) Elly de Waard represents the anecdotal school, if she represents any school at all. She has consistently rejected the iconoclasm of the self-styled "intellectuals," and helped to form a group of women poets in the late 1980s known as *De Nieuwe Wilden* (The New Savages). She sometimes employs unfashionably baroque language, and she forges direct links between language and emotions: "the feeling which belongs to / some occurrence / cannot do without / an image or a word."

We find this, too—this intimacy of feeling and word—in the work of Willem van Toorn. His poem "Two Daughters" reads, in part, from the beginning:

In the sleepy early morning
I see them as they ride
down the tree-lined track, side by side:
off to the village, A and S, my daughters.

If I was able to draw
you'd see an imprint appear before
your eyes, a picture in
which they'd be frozen: their hair, ever so thin
(they've almost reached the end,
where the road to the village begins),
blowing in the wind
under a misty sun.

Now you'll have to take
a few of my words for it. Look,
the glint of a bell or spoke.
In through the open window slides
a tight-stretched ribbon of light.

They're behind the trees. But you're seeing
their windblown hair still streaming
inside your head. . . .

Francis R. Jones, trans.

The girls' fragility, and the father's love, seem (to the speaker) to exist beyond the ability of words to express. Words, of course, are for what can be said; and we know there is much that cannot be said. However, William Stafford reminds us, "Words can do what they cannot say." And in this poem of van Toorn's, the father's animated invitations to the reader, and his acknowledgment of the limitations of language, work to do what they cannot say.

Of the hermetic school in Holland, which includes Wiel Kusters and Peter Nijmeijer, Gerrit Kouwenaar seems the preeminent practitioner. Eschewing the anecdotal, Kouwenaar strives for a cool, unsentimental lyric that is yet light enough to invite the casual reader. At the core of his work lies a belief in the inexpressibility of the world and its conditions. And yet something must be said; the inexpressibility must be approached. His poem "a waning day" reads—

It could only come from the fact that one already
knew everything, that grass sulked everywhere
where it was forbidden, that the full-fledged hedge
shut out the view, the axe had to be sharpened

that on a waning day one reviewed the distance
that the distance was closer than ever
that one had forgotten the year of the day
that the house had outlived and estranged itself

that one broke into one's entrails, the unslept-in
bed lay ready, the room had been emptied
once more saw oneself for ever for the first time

and that one felt cold and ate meat
and that the meat no longer had any taste and the fire
ignited itself and the walls warmed themselves
Deborah Ffoulkes, trans.

This poem comes from Kouwenaar's latest collection, *totally white room*, which title suggests a sickroom, perhaps, or an igloo, or a blank page—again, a kind of oblivion always lapping at the page.

A whole new generation of poets from the Netherlands, Flanders (the Dutch-speaking part of Belgium), and Surinam have taken the stage—Anne Feddema (b. 1961), Erik Lindner (b. 1968), Sieger M. Geertsma (b. 1979), Menno Wigman (b. 1966), Ilja Pfeijffer (b. 1968), and others.

Geertsma, for one, is a young white rap poet who published his debut, *Straatvluchter*, in 2002. Wigman, for another, besides having a very cool name, has played in punk rock bands, and is something of the European *maudite*; he writes out of a black romanticism, abhorring much of the banality of the modern world. Upon visiting a Burger King, he writes, "everything so low / and ugly stands so strong and firm." His poem "Night Rest" reads, in its entirety:

> *Evening. Two gardens further up spring is raging*
> *and hijackers are stealing through the dark.*
> *Somewhere nails are scrabbling for fur. Screechings*
> *for crumbs of love. Badly mangled ears.*
> *The randy hostilities of a spring night.*
>
> *Almost forgotten how I with the selfsame rage*
> *once hunted through the dark, how you still meaner*
> *than a cat sunk your nails into three hearts.*
> *How long ago that is and how lovely you still are.*

I've counted the days one by one
and with the best words that I have:
I love you. In you I find a bed.

And it is spring and we are sharing here the same
night with all that that entails.

                    John Irons, trans.

It must be ultra-modern for a poem to open with rage and hijackers and hostilities and still turn out to be a love poem. This poem narrows, stanza by stanza, to a rather lyrical couplet, actually. Wigman is said to speak for many in his generation, and perhaps he also speaks for northern Europe, coming out of the 20th century—after all the rage and hysteria, love and spring!

The northern countries have always been ultra-modern. Think of Swedish furniture. Dutch courts. Danish nudism. Even when it was uncool—think of imperialism—the northern countries were ahead of the pack. But we're younger than that now.

In Memoriam: James Still
4/28/01

James Still has died. We all thought he was going to live forever. I think maybe he thought it, too. Cresting his nineties, when some folks won't buy green bananas, he ordered journals in five-year bunches. Too contrary to die, to be rooted out of his mountains—

> *I shall not leave these prisoning hills*
> *Though they topple their barren heads to level earth*
> *And the forest slide uprooted out of the sky*
> (from "Heritage")

He used to tell people that he was born in a cotton patch. As a little boy growing up in Chambers County, Alabama, back in the nineteen-teens, he helped out the family by picking cotton and putting his in a special sack his Mama had sewn for him. Then he rode atop the loaded wagon to the cotton gin. It was there, in the fields of the Double Branch Farm, that he learned an important lesson in creativity. "One day, when I was hoeing cotton, my sister Inez began to tell a story from the next row—a true story, I thought," he wrote, in his essay "A Man Singing to Himself." His sister's story continued "for hours as our hoes chopped and pushed

103

and rang against stones. Then I learned that her story was a fabrication. She had created it while she was working. From that moment my horizon expanded into the imaginary. I could make my own tales, and I did."

He surrounded himself with tales ever after. He worked his way through Lincoln Memorial University, and went on to study at Vanderbilt with John Crowe Ransom and the Fugitives, those staunch agrarian philosophers and poets, and later Still studied at the library school of the University of Illinois. Then, his wandering days ceased when he was offered a job as librarian at the Hindman Settlement School, at the forks of Troublesome Creek, in Knott County, Kentucky, and he found a log house nearby, where he settled in to try his hand at writing. That house, over at Wolfpen Creek, had once belonged to dulcimer-maker Jethro Amburgey, and it retained some fine music—but at a pitch that only dogs and poets can hear. "One night," Still wrote, "a dulcimer hanging from a nail began to play, however faintly, but a struck match revealed a granddaddy spider walking the strings."

Still would live there for almost seven decades, time enough to put down some pretty deep roots. And that name—Wolfpen—would become a literary landmark. For it was there, betwixt mountain and creek, on the "backside of Nowhere," that James Still wrote the stories, novels, children's books and poems that have won him generations of faithful readers, and distinguished him as one of our truest native speakers. His novel *River of Earth*, alongside Steinbeck's *Grapes of Wrath*, are the two great classic works of the Depression-era America. In the 1930s, he began placing poems in all the best places—*Poetry, Sewanee Review*, the *Atlantic, The New York Times*. His reputation spread far beyond the mountains, of course. A fan letter sent him by May Swenson praised his poems, saying, "Poets today try too hard to outdo each other—they strain. Your poems are very satisfying for being simply natural." Even his short poems manage to contain a story, a narrative, and to bring forth from that story the essential images. His poem "Banjo Bill Cornett" is a good example—

> Singing he goes, wrapped in a garment of his ballads,
> And his songs are his own, and his banjo shaped
> By his own skilled hands. This is his own true love
> He grieves, these his winding lonesome valleys
> Blowing with perished leaves and winds that starve
> In the chestnut oaks, and these the deaths he dies.
> His voice is a whispering water, the speech of a dove. . . .

The simplicity of Still's poems comes from having listened and read closely. He had an attentive ear, and, from childhood on, was a voracious reader. "I suppose I've read an average of three hours a day for more than half a century," he has written. "My reading jaunts include books on the Himalayas, the South Pacific, the American Civil War, World War I, Mayan civilization, and the entire corpus of many an author. Curiosity is like an itch that needs scratching." He also traveled widely, for example, having spent fourteen winters in Central America indulging his passion for the Mayan culture. Always, his creative work was inspired by the storytelling impulse, and to include the story of his own place, Wolfpen Creek, within the world—

> I will long recall
> The maples' blossoming wings, the oaks proud with rule,
> The spiders deep in silk, the squirrels fat on mast,

The fields and draws and coves where quail and
       peewees call.
Earth, loved more than any earth, stand firm, hold fast;
Trees burdened with leaf and bird, root deep, grow tall.

Edna St. Vincent

She had hair the color of fire. A lively intelligence. And a name, her mother always said, like song—Edna St. Vincent Millay. It rolls trippingly off the tongue. Like Lo-li-ta, that other literary invention of eroticized girlhood. But, in Millay's case, she invented herself.

She preferred to be called Vincent. (The name came from the New York City hospital in Greenwich Village that had recently saved her uncle's life.) She smoked in public when it was still illegal for women to do so. She slept with men and women, and she went swimming in the nude. She wrote poems that rallied an entire generation—

> *My candle burns at both ends;*
> *It will not last the night;*
> *But ah, my foes, and oh, my friends—*
> *It gives a lovely light!*

In the depths of the Depression, Millay gave readings to standing-room-only audiences of thousands. Her collection of poems *Fatal Interview* sold out of 35,000 copies within two weeks. Her vibrant self, "her performing self, resembling a daffodil, in a long cloak and her bright hair, made people feel they had seen the muse alive and just within reach," her biographer, Nancy Milford, has written. Millay was Daphne reincarnate. A friend of hers recalled seeing her once in New York City, on MacDougal Street, running around the corner of the street with her red hair flying behind her, "flushed and laughing like a nymph," with a handsome young male friend of hers running behind, in full pursuit.

Born in 1892 in Rockland, Maine, Millay grew up in a household of women. Her mother had separated from her father, a lug of a man, but she never found the better thing she was looking for. Millay, the eldest daughter, took care of her sisters while the mother worked. Such a household still earned the disapproving stare of society. But the Millays seemed to revel in their unconventionality. When the kitchen flooded one winter, and the water froze over the floors, the girls went ice-skating through the house, hooting and hollering for all to hear. They suffered many hardships, too, primarily economic, and Millay's schooling was haphazard.

Was she destined to become a poet? She had been born with a caul, said to be a sign of eloquence. And there grew in one of her girlhood front yards a flower called *narcissus poeticus*.

Some children invent an imaginary playmate. Millay, at age nineteen, invented an imaginary lover, to whom she wrote long and tender letters. She wanted something to happen to her, "to give me a jolt, something that would rattle my teeth," she wrote in her journal, "and shake my hairpins out."

That soon happened. Accepted conditionally to Vassar College, Millay spent a year in New York at Barnard, catching up on her education. There, she met such notables as Witter Bynner (who asked her to marry him), Louis Untermeyer, Sara Teasdale, Malcolm Cowley, and Max Eastman. She was photographed by Man Ray. Edmund Wilson (who also asked her to marry him) resolved to publish her work in *Vanity Fair*, where he had recently been made an editor; it is to Wilson's credit that he fell in love with her poems before he met the poet herself. Vincent had become quite the literary socialite. Fortunately, for her, she also caught fire as a writer. Between 1917, when she graduated from Vassar, and the end of 1920, when she left New York for Paris, as a foreign correspondent for *Vanity Fair*, she published seventy-seven poems, her first book, and a play, "Aria da Capo."

Millay had herself become the thing to rattle her teeth, to shake her hairpins out. She became the first woman to win the Pulitzer Prize, and, somewhat on the strength of her unconventionality, she became a sort of American Byron, "the beau ideal of the Romantic poet," in Milford's words. Her love poems, especially, have always reminded me of another Romantic, Keats. Is not her sonnet "What lips my lips have kissed" an answering poem—personal, and intimate—to Keats' "Ode on a Grecian Urn"?

> *What lips my lips have kissed, and where, and why,*
> *I have forgotten, and what arms have lain*
> *Under my head till morning; but the rain*
> *Is full of ghosts tonight, that tap and sigh*
> *Upon the glass and listen for reply,*
> *And in my heart there stirs a quiet pain*
> *For unremembered lads that not again*
> *Will turn to me at midnight with a cry.*
> *Thus in the winter stands the lonely tree,*
> *Nor knows what birds have vanished one by one,*
> *Yet knows its boughs more silent than before:*
> *I cannot say what loves have come and gone,*
> *I only know that summer sang in me*
> *A little while, that in me sings no more.*

Too long devoted to youth, and, in herself, a youth culture, age must have come as a shock. What happened? Just yesterday, wasn't it, the world and I were young, . . .

The world and I are young!
Never on lips of man, —
Never since time began,
Has gladder song been sung

When Millay matured as a poet, she gave up the romance-angst themes, and gave voice to a burgeoning counter-tendency in her thought. Her eighteen-sonnet sequence, "The Epitaph for the Race of Man," in *Wine from These Grapes*, explores a cosmic drama, and it is prescient, written, as it was, a full decade before the atomic age and the threat of nuclear annihilation. There are no love poems in *Wine*. Here, Louise Bogan wrote in a review for *Poetry*, Millay left behind the love poetry and, as if sloughing off at last a lingering adolescence, she "crossed the line, made the break, passed into regions of cold and larger air." Writing in elegy and remembrance of her mother, Millay encompassed the cosmos—

Time, that renews the tissues of this frame,
That built the child and hardened the soft bone,
. . .
Attends no less the boy to manhood grown,
Brings him new raiment, strips him of his own.
. . .
Such hope is mine, if this indeed be true,
I dread no more the first white in my hair,
Or even age itself, the easy shoe,
The cane, the wrinkled hands, the special chair.
Time, doing this to me, may alter too
My anguish, into something I can bear.

In these sonnets, she dramatically widened the scope of her inquiries, to the end of things, and beyond. Though she gave few public performances later in her career, one can imagine her reading these darker poems, her lithe figure wrapped up in a black cloak, her flaming hair up-curled, like a torch illuminating the further reaches of emotion, in dark-bright colors such as Maxfield Parrish used, deep golds, burnt reds. . . .

Interestingly, the FBI had tracked her, though lackadaisically, ever since 1920, when she donated a dollar to a charity purchasing tractors from Soviet Russia. On the eve of World War II, the agency stepped up its surveillance of her, when she described to a reporter for the *New York Post* her disgust at "the hollow talk of disarmament." She blamed the capitalist systems of the west, saying, "I should like to live in a world where everybody has a job, leisure for study, leisure to become wiser, more perceptive." Disavowing Communism as an alternative to capitalism, she steadfastly declared, "I am intensely an individualist."

Her own favorite book? A 17th century edition of Catullus, which burned up in a hotel fire on Sanibel Island, along with an emerald ring and the manuscript of her verse drama, *Conversation at Midnight*. Her only consolation, she said, "was to say over and over to myself, *Desinas ineptire . . . et quod vides perisse perditum ducas*," from the eighth lyric of Catullus. "Cease this folly . . . and what you see is lost set down as lost."

Homage à René Char

"Barefoot, I talk to children." I write this sentence of René Char's on the blackboard, and tell my writing students that here is their challenge—to write so succinct yet magnanimous a line.

Char is one of my enthusiasms. Born in 1907, just east of Avignon, grandson of a foundling named Charlemagne, this poet of Caesar's province was allied early on with the Surrealists (Crevel and Elouard especially), then matured into a poet of great power and beauty. Whether writing lyrics or aphorisms, he never fails to startle us. He practices, soberly, Apollinaire's "hallucination of the word." His poems hum to you like a secret room in the house, that you alone find them.

Char signed Breton's anti-fascist manifesto in 1934. In 1939, as Europe darkened, he was (accurately) denounced as an anti-Fascist married to a Jew (Georgette Goldstein). He joined the *Forces Français Combattantes*, the underground French Resistance, and engaged in sabotage missions. He never lived far from his birthplace of L'Isle-sur-Sorgue, and in the 1960s he led protests against the installation of nuclear missiles on his beloved Mont Ventoux.

William Carlos Williams wrote of "the power of beauty to right all wrongs." Surely this is the siren call of art. If Char lived in a more heroic age than the present, he honored its dangers with an steady, unflinching gaze.

His literary circle included Camus, Tzara, Heidigger, Pasternak. His editions of poems were illustrated by Giacometti, Matisse, de Staël, Braque. In his writing, Char could be philosophical, then, by turn, quotidian. Prophetic, then village-simple. Sorrowful, then joyous. He wrote an essay on Braque's paintings, to accompany a 1947 exhibition at the Palace of the Popes in Avignon, and observed, "Children and geniuses know that there is no bridge, only the water that lets itself be crossed."

He kept alive a child-like wonder in his own work, magicking such prose-poetry as "Announcing One's Name"—

> *I was ten. The Sorgue enshrined me. The sun sang the hours upon the wise dial of the waters. Both sorrow and insouciance had sealed the weathercock onto the roof of the house where, together, they stood. What wheel, though, in the heart of a watchful child turns swifter, more powerfully, than that of the mill with its white fire?*
> Gustav Sobin, trans.

A poet deeply opposed to limits, he wanted each of his readers to walk "in the great spaces of the self," as he said in conversation with Mary Ann Caws, one of his many fine translators. In his poem "To Your Heart's Content," he wrote, "The poet bursts the bonds of what he touches. He does not teach the end of bonds." For him, the gods exist in metaphor, and all the earth is a garden that blooms in passionate shades of lavender and peach. Like Mistral before him—the other great Provençal poet—Char sees through to the stripe of the wood, and to the flummoxed heart of the quail.

The first time I traveled to France (not knowing much French), I bought a bilingual edition of Char's *Selected Poems* and read line by line his lovely poems of the Vaucluse——

> *Qui cherchez-vous brunes abeilles*
> *Dans la lavande qui s'éveille?*
> (Dark bees, whom are you seeking
> In the lavender awakening?)
>> Mary Ann Caws, trans.

I also read his love poems, and the odes to his native Mont Ventoux, and so I learned to rhapsodize selectively over the landscape and to whisper sweet nothings into somebody's ears, but could not ask for, nor receive, road directions. (My copy of those poems now has split into folios and single sheets, my own ink bled through and rusted, and it is held together with rubber bands.)

Traveling west from Nîmes, where he first encountered Eluard, into the vast purple hills of Languedöc, I began to record some of his aphorisms in a small brown-leather date-book of mine –

> *In my country, we don't question a man deeply moved.*
> *On my lyre a thousand years weigh less than a dead man.*
> *I invented a sleep and drank its greenness under the sway*
>> *of summer.*
> *Swift with wings too wide, wheeling and shrieking his joy*
> *as he circles the house. Such is the heart.*
>> Mary Ann Caws, trans.

I began to see the sun-drenched country-side with Char-ish eyes, and added to my list of his aphorisms some of my own——

114

The crypts exhale their one eternal breath.
An old man wipes his brow with a handful of onion-grass.
A fisherman stands knee-deep in the Gard, casting
his worries into the current.

Nocturnes on a Drainpipe

I'm meeting a friend, the poet Jan Freeman, for dinner in New York. One of us gets the restaurant wrong. So I go out looking for her. In New York City! And there she comes, riding in a horse-drawn carriage, looking for me.

———

New York City again. Fifth Avenue, in front of Bergdorf's. A youngish man sprawled on the sidewalk, behind a tin cup and a hand-lettered sign that includes the words AIDS and Homeless. The man is sobbing uncontrollably. People pass by and are stricken. Such human tragedy can scarcely be rendered in words. And yet we must try, mustn't we.

———

"Poetry is exactitude, numbers," Jean Cocteau said, "but people think that inexactitude is poetic, romantic."

———

Our neighbor was a very old man, nearly blind, who still drove. When he pulled out, we followed him with our eyes, then, when we lost him behind the hedges, we followed him with our ears. That is to say: He pulled slowly away from the curb, and aimed his black sedan at the boulevard; when we heard car horns and screeching tires, we knew that he had broached the intersection.

———————

My father drove an Austin-Healy ragtop, and he liked to hear the engine whine a little before he shifted gears. He was Muhammad Ali's doctor, when the boxer was a young amateur, and he used to take me along with him to the fights at the Armory on Saturday nights. I wandered around the elevated rings while he did whatever he did. Me, a five-year-old kid in a white oxford-cloth shirt, spending my Saturday night with fighters, promoters, gamblers, hustlers, prostitutes, etc. This went on until I came home one night and my mother noticed that my white shirt was flecked with blood.

———————

During the Second World War, the artist Marcel Duchamp climbed an internal staircase to the top of the war memorial in Washington Square, set out a small circle of Japanese lanterns, and declared the independence of a new state of Bohemia. The police arrived and chased him off, his paper lanterns flickering for hours in a light drizzle that had begun. In our own time, each of us follows his phosphorescent step through the streets to our own door.

For several days, we watched the dolphins hunting just beyond the breakers, rolling easy through the swells. This was at Folly Island, south of Charleston, where the dolphins come in close to the shore. My wife said she feels blessed whenever she sees a dolphin. That goes back a long way for her. When she was a child, her family summered here, and she would swim out a little way and sing to the dolphins, and sure enough they would come and gather round her.

———

For poetry, develop the ear. I remember a story the writer Normandi Ellis told me about her first undergraduate writing class, with Wendell Berry. It was the first workshop of the semester. Berry sat with his muddy booted feet up on the desk. Normandi read her poem. There was a long silence. Then Berry said, in that drawl of his, "Wahl, Miss Ellis, if it don't sound right, it ain't right.

———

Kay Boyle's phrase, "slim as a gondola."

———

All writing is an act of translation from the miasmic swirl of the brain into words, icons of sound. "The poem in the head is always perfect," Stanley Kunitz writes. "Resistance starts when you try to convert it into language." The true poem, then, is not its Platonic ideal. The true poem is the one that makes its way onto the page, however compromised. What we achieve, at best, is an inspired approximation. Mayakovsky's nocturne played on a drainpipe.

————

Newlyweds in the old Soviet Union used to have their photograph taken on an overlook with the Lenin hills in the background—as with so many Russian literary heroes, the individual set against the great sweep of history.

————

Politicians debate the "viability" of art, the "relevance" of art, and all the while their subtext is money. They might be surprised to learn from Joseph Brodsky that, "if what distinguishes us from the other members of the animal kingdom is speech, then literature—and poetry in particular, being the highest form of locution—is, to put it bluntly, the goal of our species."

————

The misuse of language induces evil in the soul. These words of Socrates should be displayed in every politician's office in Washington.

————

Poems dissolve time. Catullus jokes with a Marine in Riyadh. Sappho calls forth tears from a bar-maid in New Orleans.

Akhmatova nudges a British schoolgirl out of her complacency. Each reader lives in the timeless moment of the poem. It is for this reason that translators must take care not to impose their own time on the original, but rather, simply bring the original alive for their own time. When I read translations of the ancient Greeks that speak of backpacks and day-glo paints and hubcaps, I long for the clear Aegean.

————

Robert Shaw, a physicist, once remarked, "You don't see something until you have the right metaphor to let you see it."

————

The desk of Vita Sackville-West, at Sissinghurst: Crowded with memories, sets of faded books, photographs of the Woolfs, the Brontes, her husband Harold, and, in the middle, her writing stone, where she wrote or laid her head in the tired hours, the hours of struggle. Her imprint can be felt there in the stone, and, just below the surface, all those words not broken free.

Kay Boyle on the Côte d'Azur

Kay Boyle was one of the great writers and great beauties of the 20th century. Man Ray's photographic portrait shows a woman with piercing black eyes, smooth olive skin, high cheekbones and a rather severe though sensuous mouth; a black beret covers her curly dark hair. She published early on in *transition* and the other avant-garde journals of the day, and was one of the signers of *transition*'s famous Proclamation of 1929, which asserted such artistic freedoms as "The writer expresses, he does not communicate," and "The plain reader be damned."

She wrote prolifically. In the 1930s alone, she published six novels, three-short story collections, a volume of poetry, an anthology and a children's book. She lived prolifically, too. She married three times and eventually assembled a household of six children. Kay's publisher, James Laughlin of New Directions, wrote of visiting her when she was married to writer Laurence Vail, at their chalet called Les Cinque Enfants, near Megéve, France. "There was a covey of bright and handsome children, some his, some hers, with names like Sinbad, Apple, and Pegeen. A happy household." Sharon, her oldest, was born of a liason with the Scottish poet Ernest Walsh, who was the subject of Hemingway's story, "The Man Marked for Death." Not a kind story. After the birth of Clover, her sixth, in 1939, Kay would strike out the "Cinque" on the family stationery and type above it "Six." She once wrote to her agent, "Having babies is really a nice kind of relaxation, after the amount of typing one seems to do in life." Kay's third husband was the Baron Joseph von Franckenstein, by whom she had a son, Ian.

Kay's reputation as a political poet was hard-earned. As early as 1966, she traveled on a fact-finding mission to Cambodia, as part of her protest of the U.S. undeclared war in Vietnam. Back in San Francisco, she picketed the army embarkation docks, and once was arrested and taken to jail and assigned the task of scrubbing floors; she was released only when it was discovered that she was seriously ill, and she went straight into a hospital. A long-time teacher, she worried not just for the fate of the world, but also, particularly, for the young of the world:

> On the weekend, the upholstery of a sofa was replaced
> In the lobby, the gracious lobby of the Acropole
> > Palace Hotel.
> A student carried there at dawn had bled to death,
> Had bled to death on the brocade.
> > (from "A Poem for the Students of Greece")

In 1986, Kay sent me a letter at the journal I edited, *The American Voice*, enclosing a short story that had been written, as she described it, "by a student of mine whom I think is very talented. She has been a painter until last year, and a strikingly original one, and has now turned eagerly to writing. She has a book in progress, with which I am helping her. She prefers to be known as 'Abigail,' until she has had some of her writing published, and then she will use her free name...." The enclosed story proved an amazing piece of work, a tough-love mother-son story told in a naked jazzy prose. I wrote back to her straightaway, happily accepting the story for my journal. After a three-week delay—Kay had been suffering with the Taiwan flu—she sent me a curious letter. "Before another minute passes," she wrote, "I must make a confession to you. Abigail does not exist. I wanted the short stories of my daughter Apple Vail to stand on their own, and so I decided not to give her name to them. You at *The American Voice* are the first to have seen them, and both of us are so happy that you responded as you did. Can you forgive this deception on my part? . . . In a sense, she is my student, for we are devoted to each other." Apple's story occasioned a correspondence with Kay that would last until her death, in 1992.

In a subsequent letter, she wrote to say that Apple had always kept a diary—"I think this explains why her writing is painfully autobiographical." But Kay refused any share of credit for her daughter's talent, and her philosophy on this resembled closest, I think, Vedanta's rule, "A child is a guest in the house, to be loved and respected, but never possessed, for he belongs to God." To wit: Kay wrote, "I am in no way responsible for Apple's gifts as a writer, except that I gave birth to her. I never at any time 'corrected' my children's efforts at writing or other art forms, for such work was an expression of themselves at that moment in their lives."

She put me straight on another matter, too. In the same issue that carried Apple's story, I reprinted three short-short stories of Kay's that had appeared in her anthology, co-edited with Laurence Vail, *365 Days*. This book of stories, one for each day of the year, was drawn from news accounts around the world, and Kay solicited contributions from many writers—among them, Henry Miller, Raymond Queneau, Langston Hughes, William Saroyan—

but she had to write many of the stories herself. In my introduction to her three reprinted pieces, I unwittingly perpetuated an error, in saying that *365 Days* had been her idea. She wrote me to say, "Between you and me, it wasn't for a moment my idea. In fact, I shed many tears (of self-pity, of course) because there was no way I could escape involvement in the project. But I shed them when my husband would not see them. I wanted desperately to get on with my own work, but Laurence was enthusiastic about the *365 Days* project and he needed my cooperation with it, and so it was. I've always felt I lost an entire year of my own writing, but you couldn't have mentioned that in your introduction."

Kay proved a stimulating correspondent, solicitous in spite of her own busy life, always interesting, forthright with even the hardest truths. Her letter of August 1, 1987, brought the sad news that Apple, "my beloved Apple," was in a coma, due to complications following an otherwise successful surgery. Apple would rally briefly, but remained bed-ridden, and she died in May of 1988. Kay's own health declined—she was in her eighties by now—her handwriting growing ever smaller, more spidery. She finally had the cataract surgery that she had long postponed (she had not wanted to lose the time for working), but one was a botch and had to be done over. In June of 1989, she moved into a retirement home near Mill Valley, California. Because of her advanced age, she had to undergo a battery of geriatric assessment exams—though the women doctors there were outspoken about the absurdity of her being tested, for she remained lucid and sharp. "One young woman," Kay wrote, "who is going to France this summer, dispensed with all tests and questions, and said she wanted to talk about Paris instead, and so we did!" With creature comforts provided for, Kay found a renewed vigor and worked right up to the end.

In the summer of 1993, I traveled with my family to the south of France, and we stayed in a house just down the road from Vézénobres, a hilltop stone village dating from the Middle Ages. Cellars and foundations date to the 12th century. Many of the stone houses, or *bories*, have been recently rebuilt, in the traditional style—narrow low-beamed rooms behind meter-thick walls, with sturdy doors, and lace curtains and shutters at the windows. The houses, en *attouchment*, curl up the steep streets to the summit, where a *table d'orientation*, amid a ruin-enclosed field of clover, shows our relation to the immediate world: Alés to the north, Avignon to the east, Nîmes to the south, the hills of Languedöc to the west.

One day, walking the streets of Vézénobres, we noticed a remarkable painting in a potter's shop—a fantastical cityscape, in dull golds, deep reds, and royal blues, showing Moroccan-style tunnels, Greek columns, Roman arches, Russian domes, Turkish minarets, with over-sized flowers blooming through the interstices and bursting like fireworks overhead, and enormous dragonflies lazing in the air— and inquired within.

"*Un mille sanc*," the potter said.

Francs? We wondered, instinctively, now, after two weeks in country, dividing by five to figure dollars.

The potter would not take credit, but he conveyed to us that the artist herself lived just down the street, that's how he happened to have the painting hanging in his shop, and why don't we go pay her a visit? We sought out the door marked M. *et* Mme John *et* Sharon Cowling, and knocked rather too timidly. I don't think our first knocking penetrated the thick wooden door itself. We knocked again, louder. It was John who answered the door, and led us inside. He brought out wine and water and cookies. After a moment, Sharon, the author of this painting that was suddenly creating such a little stir in the village, emerged from the shadows of the house, and greeted us. White-haired, blue-eyed, speaking with a slight Austrian accent, she impressed us immediately as a consummate European, though of what nationality it remained difficult to tell.

"It did not sell in Paris," Sharon said, of the painting. "Of course, it would have sold for more in Paris!" she added with a short laugh.

She used to work, she told us, for the Ministiere du Education, in Paris, and painted on the weekends. Recently, she did well enough at an exhibit to finance their retirement move to Vézénobres; her daughter and grandchildren live in nearby Alés. Her husband, John, had been a career diplomat, British, stationed in Paris. He summed up the cultural differences this way: "The British wonder why anyone would want to live in England, and the French wonder why everyone doesn't want to live in France!"

"Isn't it the truth," Sharon added.

We chatted a bit, and eventually it emerged that I painted, Sunday-style, but mostly wrote, and edited a journal.

"My parents were both writers," Sharon said, then added, almost under her breath, "My mother was Kay Boyle."

She turned around and took down off a bookshelf a copy of *The American Voice*, the issue with Apple's story. "Apple and I were very close," she said, opening the journal, letting the pages flip past. "It meant a great deal to her that you liked and published her."

We staggered home that night, under the weight of the coincidence, and the wine, and lugging that beautiful painting. The next night, we returned for dinner, and sat out on their small terrace overlooking the valley, drinking kirs with John, while Sharon fixed a meal of tomatoes with paté, lamb stew, and strawberries in *créme fraiche*. We had brought along several bottles of the good local wine, and they were quickly gone.

Our conversation kept wending its way back to Kay—a remarkable mother, by Sharon's account. They had traveled around a good bit, and as children were always changing schools, but got passed along through the grades chiefly on the strength of her mother's worldly, learned bearing, during interviews with various headmasters.

When Sharon talked of her own brief writing career, before turning to paint, her Austrian *r* became more pronounced, and her words seemed edged with both nostalgia and disdain. "Oh, I used to write poetry. But eventually I gave it up. Too damned many rejection notes," she said, and snorted.

"Show them your books," John said.

"Oh. Alright." She left the room, and returned with several slim volumes under her arm. "I wrote poetry for years, but at last I gave it up for painting."

One of the books was a small letterpress chapbook, *Four Poems by Sharon Vail*, which had been printed privately in Paris, in 1943, by Caresse Crosby. Another was a book of photographs from the famous Beat Hotel in Tangier—of William Burroughs, Allen Ginsberg, Jack Kerouac, and, among others, the young freckle-faced eldest daughter of Kay Boyle. The third book nestled under her arm throughout the evening, and I never did discover what it was.

127

She disappeared up the stairs again, and returned with a typescript, another story of Apple's, titled "Eugenie," which had not been published. (I would read it later that night, in bed, and publish it in the fall of that year.)

As evening shaded into darkness, Sharon and John began to reminisce, to tell the old stories, not so much to us but to each other, something long-married couples do not do without a friendly audience. Memories of Eldridge Cleaver in Algiers, Malcolm X in New York, Sam Beckett in Paris, Michel Sciama at Buchenwald, James Laughlin at Megéve. . . .

At some point, Sharon switched over from wine to water, but she kept touching up my glass, and I kept up, unaware, or unwilling to let the moment end.

About the Author

Frederick Smock is a poet-in-residence at Bellarmine University, Louisville, where he received the Wyatt Faculty Award in 2005. He has published three books of poetry with Larkspur Press, with individual poems in The Iowa Review, The Southern Review, Shenandoah, and many others. He is the recipient of the Leadingham Poetry Prize and the Jim Wayne Miller Prize for Poetry. Mr. Smock is married to the writer Olga-Maria Cruz.

CPSIA information can be obtained
at www.ICGtesting.com
Printed in the USA
LVOW12s1032051117
555094LV00003B/412/P